THE ONE YEAR®

book of

Bible Promises

with poems from Ruth Harms Calkin

TYNDALE HOUSE PUBLISHERS, INC.

WHEATON, ILLINOIS

Visit Tyndale's exciting Web site at www.tyndale.com

The One Year is a registered trademark of Tyndale House Publishers, Inc.

All prayer-poems, month introductions, and devotions were written by Ruth Harms Calkin. Used by permission.

Prayer-poems were originally published in Tell Me Again, Lord, I Forget; Lord, You Love to Say Yes; Lord, I Just Keep Running in Circles; Lord, Don't You Love Me Anymore?; Lord, Could You Hurry a Little?; Lord, It Keeps Happening . . . and Happening; and Lord, I Keep Running Back to You. All copyright © Tyndale House Publishers, Inc., Wheaton, Illinois 60189. Used by permission.

Adapted versions of "Welcome Home," "The Lesson of the Windmill," "A Friendship Observed," "He Is Enough," "A Woman Who Is Real," "A Listening Heart," "Stephanie," "Three Discoveries," and "It Takes a Lifetime" were previously published in Friends, copyright © 1997 by Tyndale House Publishers, Inc., Wheaton, Illinois 60189. Used by permission.

ISBN 0-8423-3887-X

Printed in the U.S.A.

04 03 02 01 00
5   4   3   2   1

INTRODUCTION

God keeps his promises. You've heard it; in fact, you've probably even said it a few times. But how well do you know it? God's intention is for this great truth to be so foundational in your heart that you confidently live life resting in his faithfulness.

God can be trusted. Discover his promises in new ways this year and deepen your understanding of his faithfulness.

Deep in your hearts you know that every promise of the Lord your God has come true. Not a single one has failed! *Joshua 23:14, NLT*

January

The Promise of New Beginnings

Great is his faithfulness!

Morning by morning he wakens me and opens my under-
standing to his will.   Isaiah 50:4, NLT

January 1

Happy New Year

This very first day
Of the fresh new year
I sing a new song—
A joyful, exalted song!
With Israel's sweet singer I exclaim:
"How good it is to sing God's praise
How delightful and how right."
The volume increases
The tempo accelerates.
With glorious anticipation
I shout a rousing welcome
To the up-and-coming days.
The future cannot daunt me
Every inscrutable mystery
Becomes a consolation of joy
For with You in control, dear God
The worst may happen
But the best is yet to come.

Praise the Lord! Praise the Lord, I tell myself. I will praise the
Lord as long as I live. I will sing praises to my God even with my
dying breath.

Psalm 146:1-2, NLT

January 4

The Promise

God, on a long, lonely Saturday

Just before New Year's Day

You spoke so clearly through Your Word:

"Your days of mourning all will end.

You will live in joy and peace."

O God, what a glorious promise

As we begin a brand new year!

Again You said:

"Always be expecting much

From Him, your God."

I trust You implicitly, my Lord

For Your "much" exceeds by far

My greatest comprehension of much.

Surely You have planned a beautiful surprise!

I open my heart wide to receive it.

"For I know the plans I have for you," declares the Lord, "plans to prosper you and not to harm you, plans to give you hope and a future."

Jeremiah 29:11, NIV

January 5

January

It's January, Lord—

The drab, dreary middle—

And my thoughts are as drab

As the miserable month.

Does everybody hit a January slump

Or am I the only one?

The first week wasn't too bad:

There were Christmas thank-yous to write

A few resolutions to store away

The huddle of year-end sales.

But thank-you notes bring no returns

And resolutions are quickly broken

And marked-down trinkets fast lose appeal.

When You said

Behold, I make all things new

Did You forget January, Lord?

Or in January do *I* sometimes forget You?

Therefore, since we are surrounded by such a great cloud of witnesses, let us throw off everything that hinders and the sin that so easily entangles, and let us run with perseverance the race marked out for us.

Hebrews 12:1, NIV

January 6

Insight

While I was "praying," Lord
Demanding this
Insisting on that
You pierced me
With lightning-swift insight.

My bitter complaints
My self-centered whims
Do not constitute prayer
Just because they begin
"Dear God."

Your kingdom come, your will be done.

Matthew 6:10, NIV

January 7

Another Year

Another new year! How did it steal in so silently? How did it arrive so quickly? So many things I determined to do in January of last year are still completely undone. So many notes and letters still unwritten. Friends I planned to entertain were never invited. The books I planned to read haven't been opened.

The cupboards and drawers I hoped to clean are still cluttered with things I don't need or use. Clothes I no longer wear still crowd my closet. I planned to have coffee with our neighbors, but often I managed no more than a quick wave between errands.

If only I could have held on to the old year a little longer! But the old year is gone. I must put it away with all its failures and broken resolves. There is no way I can reclaim even one week of last year.

I see that the road to good intentions is wide and circular. I've walked around it until I am utterly exhausted. I confess my failures, my procrastination. I know God, in his graciousness, will forgive me. I have one more request. I pray for God's power to keep my forgiveness up-to-date.

Let me hear of your unfailing love to me in the morning, for I am trusting you. Show me where to walk, for I have come to you in prayer.

Psalm 143:8, NLT

Missing Chapter

Often, Lord

I feel achingly incomplete

Like the missing chapter

in a book.

But then I remember

You have not yet finished

The manuscript.

Forgive me

If I seem presumptuous

But have You set

A publication date?

And I am sure that God, who began the good work within you, will
continue his work until it is finally finished on that day when Christ
Jesus comes back again.   Philippians 1:6, NLT

January 9

The Choice

Lord, You are indeed relentless:

You insist that my love be unrivaled

That my loyalty be uncompromising

That my surrender be irrevocable.

What do You want, Lord

Everything?

It's frightening.

Yet not as frightening

As staying as I am.

And you must love the Lord your God with all your heart, all your soul, and all your strength. Deuteronomy 6:5, NLT

January 10

Now You Have Me, God

Now You have me, God!
You have me irrevocably.
No reserve
No retreat
No turning back.

Now You have me, God!
All I feel
Dream
Aspire
All I long withheld.
My resistance
Triumphs
Defeats
My stalwart resolves
My crumbling dreams
My glittering awards
My blind alleys.

Now You have me, God!
All which is past
All which is now
All that may yet unfold.
The barriers are broken

The turmoil has stilled
Your Word is my Yes
Your notes are my song.

Now You have me, God!
You knocked
And still knocked
And I opened the door.
Now at last—
At long last
I know:

Joy!
As the rushing sea.
Peace!
As a meadow at twilight.
Strength!
As a towering mountain.
Trust!
As a wide-eyed child
Who walks
In the gentle rain
Holding
A father's hand.

Whom have I in heaven but you? I desire you more than anything
on earth. My health may fail, and my spirit may grow weak, but
God remains the strength of my heart; he is mine forever.

Psalm 73:25-26, NLT

January 11

Make Yourself at Home

With extreme joy, Lord

I offer my heart as Your home.

I have purposely left it unfurnished

Without lavish decor:

No plush carpeting

No velvet drapes

Not even an original oil

Or an engraved silver service.

Examine it first for cleanliness—

Every room

Every closet

Then furnish it according

To Your own magnificent taste.

The door is wide open—

Don't even bother to ring the bell.

Here I am! I stand at the door and knock. If anyone hears my voice
and opens the door, I will come in and eat with him, and he with me.

Revelation 3:20, NIV

January 12

Today, Lord

Yesterday, Lord

When You asked what I wanted

Above all else

I said I wanted to be

Exclusively Yours.

Today, as You startle me

With opportunities

Keep me from begging off

Until tomorrow.

What is more pleasing to the Lord: your burnt offerings and sacrifices
or your obedience to his voice? Obedience is far better than sacrifice.
Listening to him is much better than offering the fat of rams.

1 Samuel 15:22, NLT

January 13

Unpredictable

Sometimes, Lord

You come up with such

Unpredictable answers—

Today

I related my predicament

I explained my desperation

I begged You

To get me out of this mess.

Your only answer:

"I beg you to let Me in on this mess."

Each time he said, "My gracious favor is all you need. My power works best in your weakness." So now I am glad to boast about my weaknesses, so that the power of Christ may work through me.

2 Corinthians 12:9, NLT

January 14

God's Promises Are for Keeping

Losses, depression, disappointments, frustrated desires—how debilitating they can be. This is indeed a fact. But so often we must distinguish between the facts and the promises of God. I am always helped by the Bible story of Abraham and Sarah. Sarah was too old for childbearing, but God had promised that they would have a child. So they gave preference to the promise of God, as impossible as it seemed.

In the midst of all that troubles you, all that seems impossible at times,

- God's PROMISE is: Give all your worries and cares to God, for he cares about what happens to you. (I Peter 5:7, NLT)
- The PROMISE is: I will answer them before they even call to me. (Isaiah 65:24, NLT)
- The PROMISE is: If you look for me in earnest, you will find me when you seek me. (Jeremiah 29:13, NLT)

Underline God's promises. Memorize them. Know with assurance that God has never broken a single promise, and he's not going to start with you. He wants our commitment, our obedience, and our trust. If you have surrendered to him completely, he will not fail you! Take his word for it!

All of God's promises have been fulfilled in him. That is why we say "Amen" when we give glory to God through Christ.

2 Corinthians 1:20, NLT

January 15

Suddenly Mine

O Lord

May I believe in the darkness

When all hope has vanished

When waves beat with fury

And no star lights my sky.

May I believe without

Feeling or knowing or proving

Till one shining moment when

You shatter the darkness

And all I believed for

Is suddenly mine.

Weeping may remain for a night, but rejoicing comes in the morning.
Psalm 30:5, NIV

January 16

Marvelous Moments

What a beautiful relief, dear God

To sit quietly in my own living room

Soaking up the luxury of aloneness.

No demanding voices

No radio or television

No shouts from the bathroom

Just these few marvelous moments

To kick off my shoes

Shed my confusion

And reclaim myself . . .

These few marvelous moments

To respond to Your persistent plea

"Be still and know that I am God."

You will keep in perfect peace all who trust in you, whose thoughts
are fixed on you!
Isaiah 26:3, NLT

Empower Me, I Pray

Lord, You told the impotent man

To take up his bed and walk.

Today, when mountainous problems

Seem to loom sky-high

And the business of living

Demands so much rigid attention

Empower me, I pray

To take up my task and work.

And whatever you do, whether in word or deed, do it all in the name
of the Lord Jesus, giving thanks to God the Father through him.

Colossians 3:17, NIV

January 18

You Dreamed Me Up

O dear God

It was You, You alone

Who dreamed me up.

Nobody else

Would ever have thought of me

Or planned for me

Or looked right through me

With future contemplation.

Right from the beginning of Time

I was all Your idea.

You had big things in mind for me

Good things, glorious things

And now, with magnificent dexterity

You are making them come to pass.

And I?

Well, I stand amazed on the sideline

And praise Your infinite patience.

You saw me before I was born. Every day of my life was recorded in
your book. Every moment was laid out before a single day had passed.

Psalm 139:16, NLT

Too Often

Dear, dear Lord

Too often in my life

I've messed around

In my tiny dirt plots

When through Your glorious power

I could have moved mountains.

Please change me!

Turn my eyes from worthless things, and give me life through your word.

Psalm 119:37, NLT

January 20

It's for Keeps

Lord
Even when I came to You
As a little child
Not quite nine years old
You knew the worst, the very worst
About each future sin and failure.
Still You accepted me
With Your arms wide open.
You held me close to Your loving heart
And whispered, "It's for keeps!"
Had I been an adult
You might have captured my attention
With Your cry from the Cross:
"It is finished."
But You whispered to a little girl
Who understood perfectly, "It's for keeps."

O Lord
I praise You for the liberating fact
That through all the passing years
I have never had to produce or perform
To guarantee my position in You.
It is You, not I, who maintains my status.
Nobody, NOBODY can produce an ounce of evidence
To cause You to change Your mind.
Year after year, day by day
Your words still ring in my heart:
"It's for keeps!"

The Lord himself goes before you and will be with you; he will never
leave you nor forsake you. Do not be afraid; do not be discouraged.

Deuteronomy 31:8, NIV

God's Promises

With increasing joy I am discovering that God's promises do not suddenly disappear when our courage fails and our fears become overwhelming. Feeling or no feeling, when God gives a promise that speaks directly to our need, it stands firm regardless of negative circumstances. There may be times of questioning, and we may not understand God's timing, but his promise remains certain through our deepest trial. If we consistently rely on his immutable Word, we can disregard the darkness.

Oswald Chambers says, "Are you in the dark right now regarding your circumstances? Then listen, and God will give you a very precious message for someone else when you are in the light."

God waits for us to trust him when trusting seems the most difficult thing of all.

Do not throw away this confident trust in the Lord, no matter what happens. Remember the great reward it brings you! Patient endurance is what you need now, so you will continue to do God's will. Then you will receive all that he has promised.

Hebrews 10:35-36, NLT

To Know God

O God
There is an aching longing within
  me
To know more and more
Of Your kindness and peace.
You have promised to give me
(As I learn to know You better)
Everything I could possibly need
For walking in newness of life.
By Your mighty power
You have promised to implant
Your own character within me.
But Your Word makes it clear,
  Lord
That to obtain these gifts
I need more than faith.
I must discover what You want
  me to do.
I must put aside my own desires

And strive to become patient and
  godly.
I must gladly let You have your way
  with me.
I must learn to enjoy and love
  others deeply.

You make it very clear, dear Lord
That the process is a build-up—
Addition upon addition.
But as I willingly yield to You
The reward will be the fulfillment
Of my deepest longing:
I will be spiritually strong
I will be fruitful and useful.
Above all, I will fulfill
Your divine purpose for my life.
For to know You, the eternal God
Is exactly what I was made for.

Draw close to God, and God will draw close to you.   James 4:8, NLT

Fruitless Hours

My Lord

Forgive me for spending

So many fruitless hours

Debating, analyzing, mulling over

What I think I should do

In future years—

When again and again

You have proven

That the hours of each *today*

Lived in explicit obedience

Reveal sufficient spiritual insight

To make *tomorrow* surprisingly clear!

But seek first his kingdom and his righteousness, and all these things will be given to you as well. Therefore do not worry about tomorrow, for tomorrow will worry about itself. Each day has enough trouble of its own.

Matthew 6:33-34, NIV

Something Beautiful

Here I am, dear God

Your child

A member of Your Family

Asking You

To make something beautiful

Of my life.

Yet, even as I ask

I am convinced

That the one beautiful thing

About a child of God

Is You, Jesus Christ.

So, dear Lord

As You saturate me with Yourself

My life will be beautiful.

For we are God's masterpiece. He has created us anew in Christ Jesus, so that we can do the good things he planned for us long ago.

Ephesians 2:10, NLT

For This New Year

O Lord God
You are able.

Able to make me clean
Without self-righteousness and
    sham.
Able to make me real
Without hypocrisy.

You are able
To give me wisdom
In all my priorities
My decisions, my goals.

You are able
To transform my fears
Into vibrant faith
And quiet trust.

You are able
To make this present year
The most challenging
The most productive
Of all my life.

So for this new year
I covenant with You, dear God.
Please work in me
To the very depth of my being.

Renovate me
Transform me
For You are able—miraculously
    able
To make all things new.

As the Spirit of the Lord works within us, we become more and more like him and reflect his glory even more.   2 Corinthians 3:18, NLT

I Trust

O God, thank You
That Your promises are valid
As long as the world lasts.
They do not suddenly dissolve
When my faith is feeble
And my courage fails.
When You have given a promise
You will perform it—
Sight or no sight
Feeling or no feeling.

You may take me
Through the darkest night
The deepest waters.
The very worst may happen
But out of it
You will bring the very best
For Your Word remains secure.

Lord, keep me faithful in my trust.
When I can articulate no other prayer
May my waiting heart
Continually avow:
I trust!
I trust!

Trust in the Lord with all your heart; do not depend on your own
understanding. Seek his will in all you do, and he will direct your
paths.   Proverbs 3:5-6, NLT

January 27

You Promised Me

Lord, just today I read again
The words of the prophet, Ezra.
Long years ago he prayed
"You have done what You promised
For You are always true to Your word."
My dear Lord, look into my heart.
Listen to my repeated plea.
You promised me, Lord
You promised me.
You promised deliverance
From crushing defeat.
You promised Your peace
In my aching despair.
You promised release
From agonizing pain.
I've waited so long . . . so long.
Still I cling tenaciously
To this solemn truth:
You are always true to Your word.
I trust You, dear God.
I expect to pray as Ezra prayed:
"You have done what You promised
For You are always true to Your word."

And you have done what you promised, for you are always true to
your word.
Nehemiah 9:8, NLT

God Gives the Very Best

She stood alone at the card counter reading sentimental valentines. A thousand painful memories crowded her heart. She longed to buy one special card. It seemed so right for him—as though she had written it herself.

Four weeks ago they had said a final good-bye. The break was heart-wrenching. He was so alive, so much fun, so intelligent. But day after day he stubbornly insisted he had no need or desire for God. "Let's take our moments of pleasure now," he begged.

When he proposed to her, the conflict was overwhelming. She longed to say yes, but above all else she wanted a Christian home. The wrong decision would negate all she believed about marriage.

Did she buy the card that lonely day? No, for she was convinced it would only prolong the pain. What is she doing now? She is living in daily contact with God, grateful for the gift of his peace. Since the day of her total commitment she is learning, sharing, giving—and she is trusting. She is confident that God gives the very best to those who leave the choice with him. She waits with an open heart!

The peace of God, which transcends all understanding, will guard your hearts and your minds in Christ Jesus. Philippians 4:7, NIV

January 29

Accept—Expect

My Father

Empower me to *accept*

All You have promised

And to *expect*

Every promise fulfilled.

May I never forget

How completely I am in Your hands.

Let us hold unswervingly to the hope we profess, for he who promised is faithful.

Hebrews 10:23, NIV

January 30

Be Thou Exalted

"Be thou exalted, Lord
In thine own strength;
So will we sing
And praise thy power."

Yes, Lord, Yes!
David's prayer is my prayer.

Be exalted in my day-by-day agenda
In my motives and dreams
My priorities and goals.
Even in my failures, Lord
As You turn them into stepping-stones
Toward spiritual growth.
Be exalted in my worship and praise
In my sobbing and singing.
Be exalted in my secret thoughts
My emotional responses.
Be exalted in my daily routine
The delays, the unexpected emergencies
The disappointments that often come.
Lord God, as You are exalted
In heaven and on earth
Be exalted in Your home—my heart.

Be exalted, O God, above the highest heavens. May your glory shine
over all the earth.   Psalm 57:11, NLT

Count It All Joy

Dear Lord
It is a comparatively simple thing
To face a group of hurting women
At a retreat or seminar
And share with them
The triumph that comes through suffering.
Over and over I proclaim from Your Word:
"Count it all joy."
I say it emphatically
And with genuine conviction.
But last month, dear God
When physical pain seemed unendurable
And my guarded emotions collapsed
All my carefully planned outlines
Crumbled like sand castles on a windy beach.
O God, forgive me! Forgive me!
Help me to recall often
The piercing words of Oswald Chambers:
"Our worth to God in public
Will always be determined
By our lives in private."
Teach me, dear Lord—teach ME
To count it all joy.
I have so much to learn.

Dear brothers and sisters, whenever trouble comes your way, let it be an opportunity for joy. For when your faith is tested, your endurance has a chance to grow.

James 1:2-3, NLT

February

The Promise
of Answered Prayer

Following God is something far more thrilling

than anyone has dared to dream.

Listen to my voice in the morning, Lord. Each morning
I bring my requests to you and wait expectantly.

Psalm 5:3, NLT

February 1

Another Word for Trusting

Lord, I used to think

I could prove my trust in You

By refusing to fear.

Now I see that fear

Does not dissolve

With any timid command.

Far better to cling to You

While You rebuke the fear.

Clinging is another word

For trusting.

He will cover you with his feathers, and under his wings you will find refuge; his faithfulness will be your shield and rampart.   Psalm 91:4, NIV

February 2

Longing to Please You

With all my heart, Lord

I long to please You.

But too often I lack wisdom

Or am shackled by indecision

Or deterred by incalculables.

Enable me, Lord

To relax in Your love

Released and radiantly confident

That my longing to please You

Pleases You most.

No, O people, the Lord has already told you what is good, and this
is what he requires: to do what is right, to love mercy, and to walk
humbly with your God.   Micah 6:8, NLT

February 3

Heartstrings

Lord, with no sense of direction

I'm forever losing my way.

Please tie a string

From Your heart to mine

So that even in the darkness

I'll feel the tug of Your heart

And find my way home.

He will feed his flock like a shepherd. He will carry the lambs in his arms, holding them close to his heart. He will gently lead the mother sheep with their young.   Isaiah 40:11, NLT

February 4

It's Your Move

All through the long dreary hours
Of this rough toilsome day
I have struggled to believe
That Your plan is good
That the blows and bruises
Will stablish me
That the staggering changes
Will settle me.
I have struggled to believe
That Your way is perfect.

But waiting here alone
Shrouded in thick loneliness
I confess I don't see it.
Frankly I just don't see
That Your way is perfect.
And now I hear You say
I didn't say you would see it—
I only said—it is.
So, Lord, it's Your move.
Good-night.

Oh, the depth of the riches of the wisdom and knowledge of God!
How unsearchable his judgments, and his paths beyond tracing out!

Romans 11:33, NIV

February 5

Thank You for Waiting

Had You given in to me, Lord
On the thing I wanted so much
My life today
Would be a sorry mess.

I tell You nothing new—
I simply repeat
What You told me
Long, long ago.
Finally today I see it—
From Your point of view.
Thank You for not giving in to me.
Thank You most of all
For patiently waiting
For me to give in to You.

Instantly Jesus reached out his hand and grabbed him. "You
don't have much faith," Jesus said. "Why did you doubt me?"
And when they climbed back into the boat, the wind stopped.

Matthew 14:31-32, NLT

February 6

Discovery

Lord, I have discovered

That when I try

In simple ways

To be something to others

I utterly fail

Unless You are everything

To me.

Yes, I am the vine; you are the branches. Those who remain in me, and I in them, will produce much fruit. For apart from me you can do nothing.

John 15:5, NLT

February 7

Forgiveness

Forgiveness. What does it do for us? In an amazing way it creates a fresh beginning. It lifts us out of the tangled seaweed of resentment. A miracle is performed!

It may not happen in a moment or a day. We may have to forgive at six o'clock on Monday and start over again at two o'clock on Tuesday. There is no magic wand to simplify forgiveness. Forgiveness is a deliberate setting of our will, often with no emotional high whatsoever. But once having genuinely forgiven, our soul is washed clean. We walk in dignity again. We sense a new vitality. We're no longer concentrating on hurts; we're concentrating on God.

If we would only forgive, our lives would undergo transformations beyond our highest expectations. Above all, Jesus Christ would be exalted, for it is his forgiveness that makes the difference.

Forgiveness is a beautiful word. It is God's word passed to us to use freely, joyfully. When we ask for the gift of forgiveness, God always says yes. He gave his Son to make us free, and forgiveness is the secret key to freedom.

You must make allowance for each other's faults and forgive the person who offends you. Remember, the Lord forgave you, so you must forgive others.

Colossians 3:13, NLT

February 8

Thank You for Saying No

Lord, day after day I've thanked
  You
For saying yes.
But when have I genuinely thanked
  You
For saying no?

Yet I shudder to think
Of the possible smears
The cumulative blots on my life
Had You not been sufficiently wise
To say an *unalterable* no.

So thank You for saying no
When my wantlist for things
Far exceeded my longing for You.
When I asked for a stone
Foolishly certain I asked for bread.
Thank You for saying no
To my petulant "Just this time,
  Lord?"
Thank You for saying no

To senseless excuses
Selfish motives
Dangerous diversions.

Thank You for saying no
When the temptation that enticed
  me
Would have bound me beyond
  escape.

Thank You for saying no
When I asked You to leave me
  alone.

Above all
Thank You for saying no
When in anguish I asked
"If I give You all else
May I keep *this?*"
Lord, my awe increases
When I see the wisdom
Of Your divine no.

There is more hope for fools than for people who think they are wise.

Proverbs 26:12, NLT

February 9

I Promise You Spring

O God . . . God
On this sullen winter day
When the sky is threatening
And the driving wind
Pushes against our small house
I walk from room to room
Tortured, twisted, torn.
Without a whispered warning
Without a turn or a touch
You have taken my dearest
   love—
And I am left utterly defenseless
In the cruel, crushing arms
Of intolerable grief.
I am lost and listless
Waves of despair crash over me
I am bereft of love, of joy.

Do You understand, God?
There is no splendor anymore.
There is no magic, no laughter.
There is no one who speaks my
   language
Or reads my thoughts
Or gentles my turbulent heart.
O God—there are two winters now
And the winter within me
Is by far the more dismal.
Do You understand?

Child of My love
In My infinite Plan
There are four seasons.
Trust Me . . . Trust Me . . .
I promise you—Spring.

I will never forget this awful time, as I grieve over my loss. Yet
I still dare to hope when I remember this: The unfailing love of the
Lord never ends! By his mercies we have been kept from complete
destruction. Great is his faithfulness; his mercies begin afresh
each day.

Lamentations 3:20-23, NLT

Nothing Can Separate Me

God, who or what in all the world
Can convince me that You
No longer love me—
That You've given me the slip
And thrown me over?
Shall mounting pressures interfere
With my personal relationship with
    You?
Shall shadowy fears that plague my
    nights?
Shall a palpitating heart
Or a strange buzzing in my head
Or pounding pain
Or bitter tears?

Or what if people laugh at me and
    reject me
Until I feel utterly confused and
    alone?
Or what if I can no longer work
And unpaid bills pour over me
Like a deluge of crashing bricks?
Or what if an accident incapacitates
    me
And I must depend on others for
    personal care?

Or what if I can no longer
    remember names
And my blurry eyes see double
And my hands tremble?
Or what if an earthquake crumbles
    my home
And my furniture is buried in thick
    mud?
Or what if I am left alone
Without family or friends?
Am I finished then?
Does this end my small scene?

No, dear God.
Positively not!
In all these impossible circumstances
I know that nothing is impossible
    with You.
I am utterly assured that:
In weakness or sickness
Catastrophe or anxiety
Loneliness or despair
I am Yours and You are mine.
Nothing can separate me
From Your matchless love!

And I am convinced that nothing can ever separate us from his love. Death can't, and life can't. The angels can't, and the demons can't. Our fears for today, our worries about tomorrow, and even the powers of hell can't keep God's love away. Whether we are high above the sky or in the deepest ocean, nothing in all creation will ever be able to separate us from the love of God that is revealed in Christ Jesus our Lord. Romans 8:38-39, NLT

February 11

Once and for All

Lord

May I settle it once and for all

That I am dealing directly with You.

You need never apologize

For any plan You ordain for me

Since nothing but good

Can come from Your hand.

You are sufficient

For every *changing* circumstance

In my God-planned life—

For every *unchanging* circumstance as well.

The eyes of all look to you, and you give them their food at the proper time. You open your hand and satisfy the desires of every living thing.

Psalm 145:15-16, NIV

Practice Loving

It is so simple, dear Lord
So pleasant and comfortable
To sit in church on a Sunday
   morning
Listening to a sermon about love—
Perhaps even speculating a bit
On whether my love surpasses the
   love
Of the person to my right
Or the person to my left.
But to love with Your love
To practice loving, dear God
How uncomfortable the church
   pew becomes
When I hear this ringing challenge
When I see Your gazing eyes.
Suddenly I remember the vicious
   remarks

Of the woman who misjudged me.
I remember the unscrupulous
   associate
Who finagled my husband's job.
I remember the careless driver
Who totaled our shining new car.
So quickly, Lord, I am faced
With a haunting parade
Of shameful, unloving attitudes.
God, You know me so much better
Than I know my own complex self
And still You continue to love me.
Give me, I pray, a fresh glimpse
Of Your vast, immeasurable love
For it is only out of gratitude for
   Your love
That I shall finally learn
What it means to practice loving.

Dear children, let us not love with words or tongue but with actions
and in truth.
         1 John 3:18, NIV

February 13

Reflection

Lord

Again and again I have asked You

To robe me in splendor—

To spark my life with radiance

Until there burns within me

A soft unquenchable glow.

Now today as I read Your Word

Your answer to my longing is so direct:

"They looked to him and were radiant."

Lord, the mystery is solved!

I must look steadfastly to You

For my radiance can only be

A shimmering reflection of Yours.

And all of us have had that veil removed so that we can be mirrors
that brightly reflect the glory of the Lord. 2 Corinthians 3:18, NLT

February 14

Morning Tribute

In all the years of my childhood, I doubt that we ever lived in a house where the sweet fragrance of roses didn't permeate the air.

I've never forgotten the summer ritual that made every breakfast a special event. Every morning my father would come in from the back yard with a freshly plucked rosebud—his token of love for my mother. Usually I'd be setting the table when Dad made his presentation. . . . "Here it is, sweetheart—your morning tribute."

One morning while sunbeams played leapfrog on our kitchen wall my mother stopped stirring oatmeal. She dropped her wooden spoon and threw her arms around my father. I'll never forget her words:

"There are ten thousand ways of loving and you know them all!"

Love knows no limit to its endurance; no end to its trust, no fading of its hope; it can outlast anything. It is, in fact, the one thing that still stands when all else has fallen.

If I could speak in any language in heaven or on earth but didn't love others, I would only be making meaningless noise like a loud gong or a clanging cymbal.   1 Corinthians 13:1, NLT

The Language of Love

Lord
I long so eagerly to love You more
Too often my love for You is
Cold
Calculating
Indifferent
And I so easily slip into apathy.
I dream nostalgically of might-have-beens
And often You seem a million miles away.
Frankly, I find it easier by far
To love my family and friends
Than to fervently love You.
I make this confession shamefully
And with the full knowledge
That You already know my heart's dullness.
Can You change me, Lord?
The disciples pleaded with You
To teach them to pray.
Right now I plead with You
To teach me to love.

The language of love, my child
Is always obedience
Search your heart with honesty.
Where are you shunning obedience?

But those who obey God's word really do love him. That is the way to
know whether or not we live in him. Those who say they live in God
should live their lives as Christ did.
1 John 2:5-6, NLT

Free Me Completely

O dear God
This aching desire!
My heart cries for it
Longs for it
With deep, throbbing intensity!
Yet in the depths of my soul
I know that what I ask
Is not Your highest
Or Your best for me.
I cannot come to You boldly
Nor can I make my request
In the Name of Your Son.
I dare not ask for a stone
When You offer me bread.
And so, my Lord
Though the longing clutches my heart
I yield it to You totally.
I ask not that You grant my desire
But that You free me completely
From desiring it.

Oh, what a miserable person I am! Who will free me from this life
that is dominated by sin? Thank God! The answer is in Jesus Christ
our Lord.   Romans 7:24-25, NLT

February 17

Inconsistency

Lord, forgive me

For telling You

I love You

When deep in my heart

I frantically fight

Against Your Will.

Search me, O God, and know my heart; test me and know my thoughts. Point out anything in me that offends you, and lead me along the path of everlasting life.   Psalm 139:23-24, NLT

February 18

The Infallible Test

Lord

Often I have wondered

If my love for You is genuine.

Or do I flippantly mouth it

Like a small child

Saying grace at the table?

But today as I read Your Word

I discovered the one infallible test:

"The one who obeys me

Is the one who loves me."

Lord, never again need I wonder.

You have made it plain enough.

If you love me, you will obey what I command. John 14:15, NIV

February 19

Deduction

Lord, when You say

The same thing to me so often

I surely must need it

And You surely must mean it!

Help me to take You seriously.

May I remember that the one settled proof

That I have taken you seriously

Will always be—obedience.

Those who obey God's commandments live in fellowship with him, and he with them. And we know he lives in us because the Holy Spirit lives in us.

1 John 3:24, NLT

February 20

The Exception

Lord, too often I demand

From my family and friends

More love

More affirmation

More acceptance

Than they are capable of giving.

Today, dear God

I ask You to burn this truth

Into the depth of my inner being:

Nobody in all the world

Can ever love me

As much as I need to be loved—

Except You!

For as high as the heavens are above the earth, so great is his love for
those who fear him.
                                                          Psalm 103:11, NIV

Grow Up

Picture it with me: a piece of gnarled bark tossed to and fro over the crashing breakers. First one direction, then another, back and forth, over and under. Aimless. No set purpose. Drifting . . . always drifting.

What an accurate picture of an immature Christian. Nothing but spiritual puttering. Up and down, in and out. One study group for a few weeks, then another. One church for a while, then another. Undisciplined, unsteady, one day soaring, the next day wading in self-pity. No consistency.

The apostle Paul tells us to grow up! Not grow older, but grow up into Christ. What we are today is more important to God than what we were yesterday. Our life journey with Jesus is now—this very day, this very hour. Why yearn for change if we've made no effort to follow the direction God has already given us?

To grow spiritually we must be single-minded. Our one goal? To be conformed to the image of Christ. He longs for our willingness to let him root us, cultivate us, water us. Above all, God wants our total commitment. He will take anything we give him except second place.

Don't copy the behavior and customs of this world, but let God transform you into a new person by changing the way you think. Then you will know what God wants you to do, and you will know how good and pleasing and perfect his will really is.

Romans 12:2, NLT

Only a Feeling

Lord
I don't like feeling
Like a half-person.

My child
It is only a feeling.
You are complete in Me.

Have you never heard or understood? Don't you know that the Lord is the everlasting God, the Creator of all the earth? He never grows faint or weary. No one can measure the depths of his understanding.

Isaiah 40:28, NLT

February 23

Your Word

Your Word!

O God, how it pierces

The deepest recesses of my being.

It analyzes every secret emotion

And leaves me exposed and defenseless.

At times Your Word is like fire

Burning up my pettiness, my petulance.

Or like a steady hammer

Shattering to dust my tolerated conflicts.

At other times it is like a gentle voice

Spreading great calm over my restless mind.

O Lord, I can never be content

To dabble in a chapter here and there

Or skim a verse or two

For always You confront me personally

And I know that I am looking

Beyond earth and sky

Into the very face of God.

The law from your mouth is more precious to me than thousands of
pieces of silver and gold.
Psalm 119:72, NIV

February 24

I Don't Understand

Lord

I just don't understand

What in the world

You're doing in my life.

My child

Don't try to understand.

Just live it

For Me.

"My thoughts are completely different from yours," says the Lord.
"And my ways are far beyond anything you could imagine. For just
as the heavens are higher than the earth, so are my ways higher
than your ways and my thoughts higher than your thoughts."

Isaiah 55:8-9, NLT

February 25

You Love Me

God
When I am wretched and weak
You love me.
When I am steady and strong
You love me.
When I am very right
Or terribly wrong
You love me.
When I talk too much
Or laugh too loud
Or sob too long
You love me.
When I am quiet and serene
You love me.
When I willingly obey
You love me.
When I insist on my own way
You love me.

When I fail to put You first
You love me.
When I come running back
   to You
You love me.
I need not beg You to love me
For You who are Love
Cannot exist without loving.

And yet this very day, dear God
I have no real assurance
Of Your love at all.
I wonder why?

Beloved child
The fact remains:
I love you.

See how very much our heavenly Father loves us, for he allows us
to be called his children, and we really are!   1 John 3:1, NLT

At Last

At last there is One
With whom I am perfectly safe.
One who knows thoroughly
All the rubbled ruins of my heart.
At last I see that all that is
Riddled and distorted in me
Can still find God-planned fulfillment.
At last I need no longer explore
The deep, dark forest of my thoughts
For there is One who understands me
Far better than I understand myself.
One who stands with me
In the thick of the battle
One who supports me
On the slippery, ice-crested paths.
At last I have entrusted myself
To One who guarantees my wholeness
Someone whose love is immeasurable.
In all the world He alone can love me
As I need to be loved.
At last there is One—
My Lord and my God!

My soul finds rest in God alone; my salvation comes from him. He alone is my rock and my salvation; he is my fortress, I will never be shaken.   Psalm 62:1, NIV

Lost Shepherd

Sometimes, Lord

In my groping effort to find You

I have reversed the parable

Of the Shepherd and the sheep.

In my distorted concept

The Shepherd has been lost

And the sheep have trudged down

Dangerous mountain cliffs to find him.

How sadly prone I am to forget

That I would not be searching for You

If You were not first wanting me.

Let me remember always, Lord

How foolish it is

To stumble through darkness

Searching for You

When I need only to surrender

To Your search for me.

I am the good shepherd. The good shepherd lays down his life for the sheep.

John 10:11, NLT

The Lesson

God is teaching me a valuable lesson. I am beginning to grasp that one of the marks of total surrender is the quiet confidence that God is in control. We don't come into maturity in a day, a month, or a year. When we discover that we really *can* trust God's methods, he gives us the settled confidence that every process he takes us through is worth the wait.

Waiting! The most difficult of all God's requirements! I have sometimes argued, *God, I'm not waiting for a streetcar, or for a light to change, or for the rain to stop. This is a "life issue."* In kindness he reminds me that his ways are unsearchable, unfathomable.

Slowly I am beginning to sense that in waiting I am becoming more teachable, more flexible, more discerning. As I surrender to his wise plan, as I obey his instructions, I begin to discover that what God is doing *within* me as I wait is far more significant than what I am waiting for.

So I leave it there, believing that God's sovereignty is laced with his compassion and love. He doesn't need my personal analysis!

"My thoughts are not your thoughts, neither are your ways my ways," declares the Lord. "As the heavens are higher than the earth, so are my ways higher than your ways and my thoughts than your thoughts."

Isaiah 55:8-9, NIV

February 29

Settled Decision

God, it is my settled decision

Not to choose less

When You have chosen more for me.

Not to choose the worst

When You have chosen the best.

Not to stoop to defeat

When You have provided victory.

Not to let my emptiness

Close the door to Your fullness.

I listen carefully to what God the Lord is saying, for he speaks peace to his people, his faithful ones. But let them not return to their foolish ways.

Psalm 85:8, NLT

March

The Promise of Security

Hear God's word to you:

God is our refuge and strength,

an ever present help in trouble.

I will make you as secure as a fortified wall. . . . I will
protect and deliver you. I, the Lord, have spoken!

Jeremiah 15:20, NLT

Plain Old Me

O Lord
Here I am again
Just plain old me
Coming to You
As I've come a thousand times—
And this is what always happens:
Your response is immediate
You open Your arms unhesitatingly
You draw me to Yourself
You clasp me to Your Father-heart.
Then You reaffirm my position:
I'm a child of the King
And all that is Yours is mine.
When I begin my stammering account
Of gross unworthiness
Your gentle smile hushes me.
With endless patience
You remind me once more
That my value never determines Your love.
Rather, Your love determines my value.

His son said to him, "Father, I have sinned against both heaven and you, and I am no longer worthy of being called your son." But his father said to the servants, "Quick! Bring the finest robe in the house and put it on him. Get a ring for his finger, and sandals for his feet."

Luke 15:21-22, NLT

March 2

Who Will Clap for Me?

I am often dramatic

Sometimes ecstatic

In the role I play

On the stage of Life.

I bow

And smile

And bask

In the limelight

Hoarding each moment

Of thunderous applause.

But when the curtain is pulled

For the last time

When the crowds have dispersed

And the stage is dark

Who will clap for me then, Lord?

You?

He humbled you, causing you to hunger and then feeding you with
manna, which neither you nor your fathers had known, to teach you
that man does not live on bread alone but on every word that comes
from the mouth of the Lord.

Deuteronomy 8:3, NIV

Like Now

There are black and dismal times, Lord

When there is nothing and no one but You

When encouragement from friends

(However sincere and honest)

Rings shallow and repetitious

When books seem nothing more

Than jumbled sentences

When music depresses

When food is offensive

When sleep is evasive

There are such times, Lord

Like now.

Though he slay me, yet will I hope in him.   Job 13:15, NIV

March 4

Am I Growing?

"Consider the lilies of the field

How they grow . . ."

Yes, Lord, I know

They grow *in the dark.*

Just now it is dark

Very dark, Lord.

Am I growing?

You have tested us, O God; you have purified us like silver melted
in a crucible.

March 5

Minimoods

You amaze me, Lord
Really, You amaze me.
Again and again
I bring You my minimoods:
Moods of depression
Resentment
Fear.
With every conceivable mood
I kneel in Your Presence
Sometimes impatiently
Often desperately
Always longingly.

And then—
In ways I cannot comprehend
Or possibly explain
I begin to sense
The pressure of You:
Melting
Molding
Transforming
Until minimoods of confusion
Become maximoments of silent joy.
It is too wonderful, Lord—
Much too wonderful.

Nothing is too hard for You
Not even me.

You have turned my mourning into joyful dancing. You have taken
away my clothes of mourning and clothed me with joy, that I might
sing praises to you and not be silent. O Lord my God, I will give you
thanks forever!
                                                    Psalm 30:11-12, NLT

March 6

Tell Me Again, Lord, I Forget

I don't want to get up this morning, Lord.
The day is cold and misty
I feel it
Even with the shades drawn.
My head aches
My heart skips beats
And my fingers tingle.
I just can't handle the pressure
Piled sky-high.
Lord
Do something
Say something
I'm scared.

Little one
I've already shown you
I've already told you
If you obey
You'll see.
If you refuse
I'm so sorry.

Tell me again, Lord
I forget.

The Lord hears his people when they call to him for help. He rescues
them from all their troubles. The Lord is close to the brokenhearted;
he rescues those who are crushed in spirit.   Psalm 34:17-18, NLT

March 7

Worth the Waiting

Growing spiritually is such a long, slow process! It's painful, too. Every day at the turn of the road I become acquainted with new pitfalls and heartaches. Sometimes the pain backs me into a corner. For example: There is a woman I know who is so sarcastic, so curt and unkind. Am I ever excused? Is forgiveness always a part of my growth?

So often I feel like a spiritual midget while my husband and friends appear to be spiritual giants. I seem to shrink in my own home.

Another thing: I confess I'm a coward about pain. Emotional pain. Physical pain. The pain of loneliness, the pain of grief. Yet, again and again it is true. What I must learn in my pain is that it is leading to something positive, something beyond what I can see in the present darkness.

I do want to grow! I want to become more and more like Jesus. Even though it takes so long, surely it is worth the waiting!

Grow in the special favor and knowledge of our Lord and Savior Jesus Christ. To him be all glory and honor, both now and forevermore.

2 Peter 3:18, NLT

How Else?

O Lord
I am continually amazed
At Your willingness to work
Through my nothingness
And my simplicity.
I am always suggesting
That You wait
Until some future spring or fall
When I can offer You
A more polished, glittering self—
But the very things I struggle
To correct and improve
You want surrendered as they are.
You want to give Yourself
A magnificent reputation
By Your accomplishment in me.
So, dear Lord
Take my insignificance
And make it a shining emblem
Of Your creative power.
Do it all by Yourself.

Dear child, how else
Would it ever get done?

But by the grace of God I am what I am, and his grace to me was not
without effect.

1 Corinthians 15:10, NIV

March 9

I Can't—You Can

O dear God
It comes to me
With sweet and gentle relief
That this thing in my life
Which I can't possibly handle
Is the one thing above all
That You *can* handle.
You can handle it totally
And You can handle it now.

Yes, dear child
Now let Me!

I am the Lord, the God of all the peoples of the world. Is anything too hard for me?
Jeremiah 32:27, NLT

March 10

All Will Be Well

O Lord God
In the midst of consuming sorrow
When despair and loneliness hedge me in
You understand my frailties—
My hesitancies, my fears.
As I scamper from doubt to doubt
You forgive so quickly my outbursts.
Never do You drive me away
When I rail against You
In peevish rebellion.
When I scream
"Don't You even care?"
You quiet my fragmented heart.
You work in me silently
Always planning in love.
You refine me in the white-flamed
Furnace of affliction.
In the silent darkness You whisper:
Trust Me—all will be well.

To you, O Lord, I lift up my soul; in you I trust, O my God.

Psalm 25:1-2, NIV

March 11

My Radiant Dawn

Dear God
The psalmist David said
He watched for You
As one who waits for the dawn.

I know, God
I know . . .

One who waits for the dawn
Waits in quivering darkness
In loneliness
In somber silence . . .
He waits for that
Which comes slowly—
Ever so slowly . . .
But, God
He waits for that
Which he *knows* will come
And when it comes
At last there is light!

I am waiting
As David waited.
O God
You *will* come—
My Radiant Dawn!

My soul waits for the Lord more than watchmen wait for the
morning, more than watchmen wait for the morning.   Psalm 130:6, NIV

At This Very Moment

O God

At this very moment

When I feel utterly abandoned

When I feel You are an enemy

And not my friend

When I feel You have turned Your face

And withdrawn Your love

At this very moment

I throw myself into Your arms

And stubbornly refuse to move.

What will You do with me now?

I waited patiently for the Lord to help me, and he turned to me and heard my cry. He lifted me out of the pit of despair, out of the mud and the mire. He set my feet on solid ground and steadied me as I walked along.

Psalm 40:1-2, NLT

March 13

Just Come Home

God, You are so good!
When at last I called to You
From my prison without Exit
You did not exact from me
A solemn promise to do better.
You did not insist
That I adhere to an endless set of rules
To guarantee Your acceptance of me.
Nor did You say with frightening sternness
"Stand on your own two feet."
Rather, with breathtaking simplicity
You unlocked prison doors
You invaded the very depths of me
You encompassed me with transforming love.
On the very spot where I groped and grappled
You turned me about toward a rugged cross.
You pointed to an empty tomb.
Then with gentle urging You said
"Your past is obliterated
Your future is secure
Just come home!"

He is so rich in kindness that he purchased our freedom through
the blood of his Son, and our sins are forgiven. He has showered
his kindness on us, along with all wisdom and understanding.

Ephesians 1:7-8, NLT

March 14

Has God Passed Me By?

We were sitting in our living room before a cheerful hearth fire, listening to the low March wind beat against our house. My pretty seventeen-year-old friend looked pensive. She said finally, "You'll probably think I sound morbid, but sometimes I just get the feeling that God has passed me by. He just doesn't seem personal. It's like being all alone in a huge computer universe where I don't really matter."

The doubts of a seventeen-year-old? If we're honest we'll all confess that we're prone to ask questions: Why life's tragedies? Why disease and pain and heartache? Why the sense of futility so often? Does it really matter to God about me?

What better evidence than the Cross? What better evidence than the Lord's promise, "I will never leave you nor forsake you." Our vast universe is in God's control. We are not governed by fate, but by our Father. Not chance, but his choice. Not a guessing game, but his guidance. He chose us to be the objects of his lavish love.

Cast down, perhaps—that we might learn to trust, regardless of circumstances. Tested, that we might claim God's unlimited resources. Passed by? Never!

God has said, "Never will I leave you; never will I forsake you." So we say with confidence, "The Lord is my helper; I will not be afraid."

Hebrews 13:5-6, NIV

March 15

It's Good

God, it's good to be loved by You!

The breathtaking knowledge

Of Your life-giving love

Rings chimes in my tremulous heart.

It fashions eternal declarations

Out of unsettled questions.

It creates a majestic life symphony

From a solitary note.

God, it's good to be loved by You!

I will sing of the Lord's great love forever; with my mouth I will make your faithfulness known through all generations.   Psalm 89:1, NIV

March 16

The Mountain

Dear Lord

I see it more clearly now:

Again and again I've begged You

To remove my mountain of difficulty—

While You have been patiently waiting

To cleanse my cluttered doubts

And calm my frantic fears

So I may climb the mountain.

For I can do everything with the help of Christ who gives me the strength I need.
Philippians 4:13, NLT

The Exchange

O God
You are continually
Stripping me . . .
Stripping me . . .
Of all my natural plans
My dreams
My successes
My secret ambitions.
For so long, Lord
My natural achievements
Have been my one consuming thought.
And now they lie before me
In a paltry heap.
God, why?

My child
It is the only way
I can begin to shower you
With all the joys
Of the supernatural.
Do you resist that exchange?

Turn my heart toward your statutes and not toward selfish gain. Turn
my eyes away from worthless things; preserve my life according to your
word.
Psalm 119:36–37, NIV

March 18

What Is Your Schedule, God?

Lord
Many years ago Martin Luther said
"It is God's nature
To make something out of nothing.
That is why God cannot make anything
Out of him who is not yet nothing."

In ways I had never anticipated, Lord
Slowly but persistently
You continue Your hammering and crushing
In every hidden crevice of my life.
You seem determined
To reduce me to nothing
In order to make me something.
I wonder . . .
What is Your schedule, God?
As You creatively continue
To reshape and remake me
How long will the process last?
Lord, could You hurry a little?

And I am sure that God, who began the good work within you, will
continue his work until it is finally finished on that day when Christ
Jesus comes back again.   Philippians 1:6, NLT

How Is It, Lord?

How is it, Lord?

My friend is able
To speak with amazing assurance
About Your sustaining comfort
In times of heart-throbbing grief.
She expounds magnificently
About Your shining presence
In times of fear and despair.
Her smiling declarations
About Your healing power
In the midst of tormenting pain
Are intended to encourage, I'm sure.
But I'm puzzled, Lord.
How can she speak so confidently
When she is so comfortably settled?
When she has never lost one
More precious than life to her?
When her greatest obstacle
Is her lack of discipline?
When by her own admission
She has never been sick
A day in her life?

O Lord . . . ever-patient Friend
Forgive me for the times
I have foolishly attempted
To offer the solace
That You alone can give.

To all who mourn in Israel, he will give beauty for ashes, joy instead
of mourning, praise instead of despair. For the Lord has planted them
like strong and graceful oaks for his own glory.   Isaiah 61:3, NLT

March 20

When Trouble Comes

My Lord . . . my dear Lord
Again this morning
As I read the words of the Psalmist
You refreshed my heart
And replenished my hope:
*"When trouble comes He is the place
   to go."*

Trouble!
Always I am unnerved
By its unannounced entrance
Into the secret corridors of my
   soul.
Pushing through with frightening
   force
It comes in sinister shapes and
   sizes.
I am never prepared for its
   onslaught.

Trouble!
Fashioned as pain it overwhelms
   me.
As sorrow it grieves me.
As disappointment it numbs me.

As failure it defeats me.
As anxiety it entangles me
In a perilous net of depression.

But God
I have boldly underlined David's
   words:
*"When trouble comes He is the place
   to go."*
How foolish to go running
From friend to friend
From place to place
When You have promised to
   deliver me.
It is in Your proximity
That my frantic fears dissolve.

*"When trouble comes, He is the place
   to go."*
In the margin of my Bible I have
   written:
Yes!
Yes!
Yes!

The Lord is a refuge for the oppressed, a stronghold in times of
trouble. Those who know your name will trust in you, for you, Lord,
have never forsaken those who seek you.   Psalm 9:9-10, NIV

March 21

The Truant

What does God do with a truant who plays hooky from her heavenly Father? What are the options? One thing is sure: He doesn't pamper her. He knows she needs to stretch her spiritual muscles.

He doesn't shout, "Get up, foolish child!" She's so covered with mud she can't move. He doesn't condemn her, because his promise is "There is therefore now no condemnation."

In the end he does what he always does for any half-demolished child of his: He unlocks her handcuffed spirit with his key of infinite love. He checks her fluctuating heart with its spiritual irregularity. He gives her a fleeting glimpse of things as they could be. He accepts her confession. He thoroughly cleanses her, then he holds her close to his tender heart. He restores her joy and empowers her to obey.

Suddenly she knows with great gladness that her one safe fortress is the center of her Father's will.

At least so it is with one truant child: *me*.

If we confess our sins to him, he is faithful and just to forgive us and to cleanse us from every wrong. If we claim we have not sinned, we are calling God a liar and showing that his word has no place in our hearts.
1 John 1:9-10, NLT

March 22

I Will Wait

O Lord
Today I must face it honestly with
 You
By pursuing the persistent
 questions within me:

God, is there any gain at all by my
 doubting?
Do doubts make me stronger?
Do they purify my heart? Fortify
 my will?
Are my emotions firmly
 established by my doubts?
Are my family and friends
 encouraged?

On the other hand, God
Even though I see no possible way
 out
Of the catastrophe I now face
Is there anything more pleasing
 to You
Than my personal choice to trust
 You?

I know it is true, Lord
I must rely on Your promises
 in the end.
Would You be glorified, dear
 God
If I trusted You now at the early
 beginning?

O God, forgive me
For so limiting You.
Surely You know exactly what You
 will do.
You are God, so You will not alter
 Your Word.
Your power is instantly operative
In all the strange twisting of my
 life.
You are God, so You are good.

I will hope
I will trust
I will wait
On the living God!

Yet the Lord longs to be gracious to you; he rises to show you compassion. For the Lord is a God of justice. Blessed are all who wait
for him!

Isaiah 30:18, NIV

March 23

By You, Dear God

To be tattered and torn
Bit by bit, day in, day out
Or to be shattered totally
Like a crystal goblet
Flung fiercely against a giant rock.
To know the brutal intensity
Of pain and despair.
O God
How unbearable it seems
How intolerable as it happens.

But finally, finally
To stand against the storm
To stretch with the strain
To accept the pain
With a measure of quiet hope.
To look beyond the intrusion
And above the confusion
To catch a glimpse of rainbow
In an ocean of tears . . .

O great God
This is to trace at last
Your guiding hand—

To sense Your gentle touch.
This is to know Your presence—
More precious than
    understanding—
To know Your compassion
Persists through the darkest night.
This is to walk courageously on
In the midst of a desolate
    wilderness.
This is to be loved
To be held
To be kept
By the Sustainer of the universe.

To be loved
To be held
To be kept
By You, dear God
By You!

Those who live in the shelter of the Most High will find rest in the
shadow of the Almighty. This I declare of the Lord: He alone is my
refuge, my place of safety; he is my God, and I am trusting him.

Psalm 91:1-2, NLT

March 24

I Know You Best

God

So often I have

Seen and heard You

Between smiles

And singing

And laughter.

But I am beginning to see

I learn to know You best

Between sobs.

No discipline is enjoyable while it is happening—it is painful! But afterward there will be a quiet harvest of right living for those who are trained in this way.

Hebrews 12:11, NLT

At Such Times

God, there are times
In the midst of heartache and heartbreak
When there is no comfort, no solace
Anywhere at all.
There are times
When in my crumbling state of mind
I feel I can no longer endure—
Not for a day, not even an hour.
It is at such times, O God
That I draw heavily
Upon Your unfathomable love.
At such times I implore
Your transforming peace.
At such times I live
By the power and promises
Of a Father who cares infinitely more
Than I can begin to grasp or comprehend.
Today, dear God, is a "such time."

Do not be afraid or discouraged, for the Lord is the one who goes
before you. He will be with you; he will neither fail you nor forsake
you.

Deuteronomy 31:8, NLT

March 26

Wrong Question

My faithful God

I see afresh this morning

The grave error of my question

"Don't You love me anymore?"

I ought always to ask instead

"How can You love me so continually

With such immeasurable love?"

Praise the Lord, all you nations; extol him, all you peoples. For great is his love toward us, and the faithfulness of the Lord endures forever. Praise the Lord.   Psalm 117:1-2, NIV

God, Why Do You Hide?

O God

Why do You hide from me

When I need You so much?

Why do You make it so difficult

For me to find You

When I know You are there?

When You have given me

Great and glorious promises

Why are none of them fulfilled?

When loneliness overwhelms me

Where is Your hand?

When I am depleted with fatigue

Where is Your rest?

O God, why do You hide from me?

Child of many questions

How can I answer

When you never stop asking?

Be still, and know that I am God.

Psalm 46:10, NIV

March 28

Wonderful Joy Ahead

During the last three months of my mother's life, I was the willing caregiver for her as she battled a malignancy that seized her with brutal force. It robbed her of her zest, her gentle charm, her quick wit. I often walked aimlessly from room to room, pleading with God to release her from the intolerable pain.

Yet, in the midst of my mother's suffering, she called me to her bedside to remind me that Peter had told the early Christians to be truly glad—there is wonderful joy ahead, even though the going is rough down here for a while.

Frankly I could feel nothing of the wonderful joy ahead. I wanted an answer now.

Then one day when the pain subsided slightly, Mother began to pray aloud. I shall never forget her prayer: "God, I don't know how to interpret the sudden changes that have come so swiftly, nor can I explain the disappointment when so many plans seem unfinished. But I can still believe that to those who love you, you *always* bring ultimate joy." Then, with a kind of spiritual exuberance she added, "And dear Lord, you *know* how much I love you!"

At that moment I saw anew that though there are no pat answers, there is one who is the Answer—the Lord Jesus Christ!

We know that in all things God works for the good of those who love him.
Romans 8:28, NIV

March 29

I Often Forget

God

In the night's darkness

When sleep is evasive

I try with some semblance of clarity

To talk to You.

But I am troubled, dear Lord

After sleep finally beckons me

For by morning I often have forgotten what I prayed.

Never fear, weary child.
Though you forget
I always remember.

Can a mother forget the baby at her breast and have no compassion
or the child she has borne? Though she may forget, I will not
forget you! See, I have engraved you on the palms of my hands.

Isaiah 49:15-16, NIV

March 30

God, How Can I Describe You?

O God

How can I describe You?

To whom can You be compared?

Your Word says

No one in all the world

Can begin to fathom

The depths of Your understanding.

You sit above the circles of the earth.

You stretch out the heavens like a curtain.

You count the stars

To see that none of them have strayed.

You pick up the islands

As though they had no weight at all.

So why should I grapple

With a single lingering doubt

That You are powerful enough to hold me?

Look up into the heavens. Who created all the stars? He brings them
out one after another, calling each by its name. And he counts them
to see that none are lost or have strayed away. O Israel, how can you
say the Lord does not see your troubles? How can you say God
refuses to hear your case?
                                             Isaiah 40:26-27, NLT

March 31

The Question

Yes, Lord, I know.

This is the way it will always be.

When You give me a definite promise

It is never a question

Of what *You* will do.

It is always a question

Of what *I* will do.

Without a single doubt

You will always keep Your word.

The question is—

Will I believe You?

"If you can?" said Jesus. "Everything is possible for him who believes." Immediately the boy's father exclaimed, "I do believe; help me overcome my unbelief!"

Mark 9:23-24, NIV

April

The Promise of Peace

God promises:

He will keep in perfect peace

all those who trust in him.

Jesus said, "Come to me, all of you who are weary and carry heavy burdens, and I will give you rest. Take my yoke upon you. Let me teach you, because I am humble and gentle, and you will find rest for your souls."

Matthew 11:28-29, NLT

April 1

Winner

Lord
How did it happen
That You chose me
To belong to You?
Whatever the reason
One thing is certain:
I won.

You did not choose me, but I chose you and appointed you to go and bear fruit—fruit that will last. John 15:16, NIV

April 2

Walking Together

It would be sheer mockery, Lord

It would be subtle hypocrisy

For me to kneel

Anguished and weeping

Before Your Cross

Unless—

As I walk with You now

Down my personal Emmaus Road

I introduce You

With singing joy

To the broken and bound

The weary and worn

The depressed and defeated

Whom we meet on the way.

And, Lord, I observe

That as we walk together

Foot traffic thickens.

The King will reply, "I tell you the truth, whatever you did for one of the least of these brothers of mine, you did for me." Matthew 25:40, NIV

April 3

Eradication

Lord

I can no more

Eradicate my own guilt

Than I can

Sit on my own lap.

You alone can cleanse me.

While You accomplish the impossible

May I sit on Your lap?

Thank You for holding me, Lord.

I like it here.

My dear children, I am writing this to you so that you will not sin.
But if you do sin, there is someone to plead for you before the Father.
He is Jesus Christ, the one who pleases God completely. He is the
sacrifice for our sins. He takes away not only our sins but the sins of
all the world.   1 John 2:1-2, NLT

April 4

No Compromise

Walking home through fog and mist
Still pondering
Still puzzled and unsure
I desperately hoped we'd settle it.
That's why I said
"When I *know* I'll *do*."

But You wouldn't drop it, Lord
Not for a minute.
In fact, Your response was firm:
"When you *do* you'll *know*."

Then with soft gentleness You asked:
"When did I fail you last?"

By faith Abraham, when called to go to a place he would later receive
as his inheritance, obeyed and went, even though he did not know
where he was going.   Hebrews 11:8, NIV

April 5

My Delight

"You are My Delight . . ."

This, dear God

You said to Jesus

At the moment of His baptism

There in the river Jordan.

He is Your Son

I am Your child

Forever related to You through Him.

Baptize me, dear God

In the river of Your Love

Your Joy

Your Power

Until with deep and widening gladness

You can say to me

Your chosen child

"You are My delight."

The Lord delights in those who fear him, who put their hope in his unfailing love.   Psalm 147:11, NIV

April 6

Who Am I?
(Acts 17:28)

In Him
I live
I move
I have my being.
Therefore
Who am I?
I am in God.
In the
Great *I AM*
I am.

Thank You, Lord.
At last
I know
Who I am.

Therefore, if anyone is in Christ, he is a new creation; the old has
gone, the new has come!   2 Corinthians 5:17, NIV

The God of Miracles

When she asked to speak to me, I noticed her glowing eyes. "Ruth, I just want to tell you that the God of miracles has worked an incredible miracle in my troubled heart.

"For weeks I attempted to force from God's control that which belongs only to him: *Vengeance!* Flames of resentment burned within me. With clenched fists I wanted to retaliate. Frankly, I hoped the offender was miserable! My words became stuttering syllables. I realized that the bondage of my own making was crippling my soul.

"Then one gray morning, without really thinking, I opened my Bible at random. The words on the page were clear and distinct: ' "It is mine to avenge. I will repay," says the Lord.'

"I was gripped with conviction. Suddenly I knew that healing was impossible unless I totally surrendered the pain to God. Slowly, my clenched fists became open hands. In a way I cannot explain, I began to pray for the one who had wronged me. I prayed with honest forgiveness.

"In a way I cannot explain, the flames of anger became charred embers. I was free! God took my sadness and gave me his gladness. He is indeed a God of miracles!"

Dear friends, never avenge yourselves. Leave that to God. For it is written, "I will take vengeance; I will repay those who deserve it," says the Lord.

Romans 12:19, NLT

April 8

My Only Defense

The powerful reality grips me,
    Lord
That when I kneel in Your
    presence
To ask Your forgiveness
I am utterly stripped of facade.
You accept no big-name
    references
No high-caliber
    recommendations.
Extenuating circumstances
Crumble to dust
In Your court of appeal . . .
I am forgiven never
Because of inherited tendencies
Or emotional discomfort
Or nagging weakness . . .

I can never plead
Corrupt environment
Or life's strange twistings
Or my own unbelievable
    stupidity . . .
Ultimately I have one solitary
    defense.
Only one—
But always one:
Forgive me, God
For Jesus' sake.
Like a song unending
The words keep singing . . .
I am totally forgiven
I am continually cleansed
Just for Jesus' sake.

Then I said, "My destruction is sealed, for I am a sinful man and a member of a sinful race. Yet I have seen the King, the Lord Almighty!" Then one of the seraphim flew over to the altar, and he picked up a burning coal with a pair of tongs. He touched my lips with it and said, "See, this coal has touched your lips. Now your guilt is removed, and your sins are forgiven." Isaiah 6:5-7, NLT

All Gone

Thank You, Lord

For cleansing my heart's wound

With Living Water.

Thank You for Your bandage

Of pure, gentle love.

Thank You for the kiss of comfort.

At last the hurt is gone.

Praise the Lord, I tell myself, and never forget the good things
he does for me. He forgives all my sins and heals all my diseases.

Psalm 103:2-3, NLT

Limping Home

Lord
With a crooked stick for a cane
I'm limping home.
Mocked and maligned
Stooped and stupid
Soiled and shabby
I limp toward You.
You could say, "I told you so."
You could say, "It's a little too late."
You could say, "Wait while I think it over."
You could sweep me under the rug—
We both know I deserve far less.
But when I see the Cross
And the Man who died there
Suddenly I know I limp
Toward unfathomable love
And there is forgiveness
Rushing toward me.
I don't ask for a banquet, Lord
Nor do I need a gold ring.
I'm so hungry
So thirsty
For You.

Then Jesus said, "Come to me, all of you who are weary and carry heavy burdens, and I will give you rest." Matthew 11:28, NLT

Change of Heart

One night
In black and bitter agony
I cried, "No, Lord!
No! No!"
Then suddenly
I saw Your Cross.
I saw You enduring
Intolerable pain.
I saw the nails
The thorns
The drops of blood.
I saw Love
Nailed willingly to a tree.
Slowly, slowly
My turmoil melted
Until at last
My throbbing heart sobbed
"Yes, Lord!
Yes! Yes!"

I will give you a new heart and put a new spirit in you; I will
remove from you your heart of stone and give you a heart of flesh.

Ezekiel 36:26, NIV

I Love It, Lord

What in the world
Is going on today, Lord?
Why the big celebration?
The fragrance of lilacs
The shimmering sound of birds
The red-gold sky
The air blue and sweet
The sudden burst of pink bloom
A thirsty vine
The shout of mountains miles around . . .
Really, Lord
What's happening?

Is it—
Could it be
That Spring has made her debut?
Is that why
You've dressed all of Nature
In party clothes?

Whatever the reason
I love it, Lord.
Thank You!

Let them all praise the name of the Lord. For his name is very great;
his glory towers over the earth and heaven!   Psalm 148:13, NLT

Greater Than Sin

Lord, never before today

Have I so deeply understood

The ugliness of my sin.

But never before today

Have I been so completely submerged

In the ocean of Your grace.

But God showed his great love for us by sending Christ to die for us
while we were still sinners. Romans 5:8, NLT

April 14

Easter Keeps Happening

Who can predict a single day ahead? (Isaiah 43:9)

The prophet Isaiah's question is agonizing. Who can? In one sweeping moment an ordinary day can become a grotesque nightmare. It can shatter our composure and torment us with grief. Adversity strikes when we least expect it. Seldom are we warned, never are we prepared.

But the chapter in Isaiah goes on to say, "From eternity to eternity I am God." This is the one glorious assurance. In the midst of a thousand puzzling questions, God is, he knows, he sees, he loves. The mysteries of both life and death are in his capable hands.

There is never a shortcut to the end of grief. Slowly, gradually it moves. We wait, even when waiting seems intolerable. The Bible explains it only partially. Jesus himself is our only complete explanation. Someday we will see beyond the mystery that now we must trustfully accept.

The glorious truth is—Jesus *did* walk out of the tomb. Easter keeps happening . . . and happening! We look ahead with glorious hope.

"You have been chosen to know me, believe in me, and understand that I alone am God. There is no other God; there never has been and never will be. I am the Lord, and there is no other Savior. First I predicted your deliverance; I declared what I would do, and then I did it—I saved you. . . . You are witnesses that I am the only God," says the Lord. "From eternity to eternity I am God."

Isaiah 43:10-13, NLT

April 15

Easter Morn

It was early dawn, Lord
And I was looking for You.
Looking
Looking
And weeping.
Within the dismal tomb
I searched
I called
I waited
But nowhere could I find You.

Then through the gray
There came a vibrant voice:
He's risen!
He's alive!
Rush toward joy!
You'll find Him everywhere
Outside the tomb—
But never, *never* there.

Startled and amazed
I left the tomb
To walk the path of praise—
Then looking up
I saw You by my side
And all of life became
An Easter morn.

You will go out in joy and be led forth in peace; the mountains and hills will burst into song before you, and the trees of the field will clap their hands.

Isaiah 55:12, NIV

April 16

Discoveries

Lord God

Today You have penetrated

My entire being

With three glorious discoveries:

When I am most weak

You are most strong.

When I am most fearful

You are utterly faithful.

When I am at my sinning worst

You are at Your saving best.

What can we say about such wonderful things as these? If God is for
us, who can ever be against us?
Romans 8:31, NLT

I Have a Father

Lord, it was one humdinger of a
  fight.
I wondered if it would ever end.
But three solid blows later
Little Loser limped toward his
  home.
With his fists clenched he shouted:
"I'll tell my father on you!"
(I had a feeling he meant it.)
Then all of a sudden it happened—
Out the front door he walked
Calm and serene
His tall hefty father by his side.
Like a streak of jagged lightning
His frightened opponent was on
  the run.

O Lord, what a reflection of me.
I too must do battle
With the adversary of my soul.
At times he comes masked
As an angel of light.
He thwarts and antagonizes.
He blinds and binds.
He harasses and accuses.
I'm no match for him, Lord.
The battle wages against
Principalities and powers.

But the great triumphant truth is—
I have a Father.
My Father protects and upholds
  me.
He strengthens and supports me.
Nothing can happen to me
Outside my Father's will.
My Father is greater by far
Than he who is in the world.
Once and for all it was settled
On a rugged cross
On a lonely hill:
I have a Father.

And I will be your Father, and you will be my sons and daughters,
says the Lord Almighty.   2 Corinthians 6:18, NLT

April 18

So Profound

O God

I want to sing and dance

I want to shout it from the hilltops:

There is absolutely nothing

In my wretched past

That can hinder You

From redeeming my future

Except my refusal to let You.

Thank You for invading my heart

With a truth so refreshing

So magnificent

So profound!

All honor to the God and Father of our Lord Jesus Christ, for it is by his boundless mercy that God has given us the privilege of being born again. Now we live with a wonderful expectation because Jesus Christ rose again from the dead. For God has reserved a priceless inheritance for his children. It is kept in heaven for you, pure and undefiled, beyond the reach of change and decay.   1 Peter 1:3-4, NLT

April 19

There Is Easter!

Death seems so wrong, dear Lord
Couldn't You have remedied it?

Have you forgotten, dear child?
There is Easter!

I will ransom them from the power of the grave; I will redeem them
from death. Where, O death, are your plagues? Where, O grave, is
your destruction?   Hosea 13:14, NIV

April 20

Ask Me Anything

I have to say it, Lord—
I just have to say it:
Sometimes You seem to be
Extremely inquisitive.
In orderly sequence You ask . . .
How are you spending your time?
What are your spiritual goals?
Why do you harbor secret
   resentment?
Where are you growing in depth?
When will you put Me first?
Lord, is nothing personal or
   private
In my day-by-day living?
Must I continually expose my
   heart?

Are You forever the "Hound
   of Heaven"
Seeking me out
Searching, sorting, pointing?

Child of my constant concern
If I withdrew from you
Leaving you totally alone
Would you be pleased?

O dear God
No, no!
Ask me anything—
Anything at all
But never let me go!

For the word of God is full of living power. It is sharper than the
sharpest knife, cutting deep into our innermost thoughts and desires.
It exposes us for what we really are. Nothing in all creation can
hide from him. Everything is naked and exposed before his eyes.
This is the God to whom we must explain all that we have done.

Hebrews 4:12-13, NLT

April 21

Even This

It was a long letter—pages of tear-stained script. "Even God doesn't care. . ." she wrote.

Perhaps you haven't put it in a letter, but has some overwhelming failure or fear obscured your sense of God's presence?

That was the catastrophe of the frightened disciples. The wind was boisterous, they had lost control . . . and Jesus went on sleeping.

We quickly identify with the shouting: "Don't you even care if we go under?" We've all shouted it, at least in attitude. Jesus quieted the sea that night, but his piercing question hits the target of our hearts: "Don't you *even yet* have confidence in me?"

The awe-filled disciples said among themselves, "Even the winds and the seas obey him."

"How wonderful," we say.

Then suddenly, often without warning, the winds of adversity beat against our personal lives, and we cry "*Lord, don't you even care?*"

Again he asks, "Don't you *even yet* have confidence in me? That habit that chains you. That fear that paralyzes you. That loss that numbs you . . . even this—*all of this* you may fling upon me!"

But it means more than half-heartedly singing, "He will break every fetter." It means surrendering to him completely. He knows your *every* need—*even this.*

[Jesus] rebuked the wind and said to the water, "Quiet down!" Suddenly the wind stopped, and there was a great calm. And he asked them, "Why are you so afraid? Do you still not have faith in me?"

Mark 4:39-40, NLT

April 22

Ecstasy of Joy

O dear God

What ecstasy of joy

That You took the whole of me

And made me wholly Yours!

You have made known to me the path of life; you will fill me with joy in your presence, with eternal pleasures at your right hand.

Psalm 16:11, NIV

April 23

The Secret

I couldn't help but watch her
As we sat in the service together
Last Sunday morning . . .
Her white hair so neatly coiffured
Her hands resting on her open Bible
Her smile so beautifully tranquil.
When the hymn was announced
She sang with a glowing smile.
Occasionally during the message
She nodded her head in assent.
(O Lord, what peace she portrays.)
After the service I spoke to her:
"You are an inspiration, my dear.
I hope I may sit with you again."
She thanked me profusely.
Then she added with shining joy
"Isn't it wonderful to know Jesus?
I mean—really KNOW Him!"
In that instant, dear God
I knew the secret of her radiance.

Yes, everything else is worthless when compared with the priceless
gain of knowing Christ Jesus my Lord.   Philippians 3:8, NLT

April 24

Long-ago Memories

Tonight, long-ago memories

Have been wandering down

Old familiar streets

And dark alleys

And dimly lit corridors.

With stubborn tenacity

They invade my carefully guarded defenses.

Sitting all alone watching dreams go by

I discover unexpectedly

That I am still susceptible to tears.

And then I recall vaguely

Part of an old song that says

"For these tears I died"

And my yearning heart, dear Lord

Reaches out for You.

Gladness and joy will overtake them, and sorrow and sighing will flee away.

Isaiah 35:10, NIV

April 25

My Personal Rainbow

Lord, right now
I struggle with clutching fear.
Waves of agony pour over me
As I face the darkest moments
In my life's history.
But my conviction still stands firm:
You are my God!
And though I cannot predict my future
Or even tomorrow
I am sustained by the reminder
That the longest storm
The world has ever known . . .
And the worst . . .
Came to an end one clear-sky morning.
It was true for Noah
It will be true for me.
Though as yet I see no deliverance
I watch
I wait
I expect
My personal rainbow.

And we know that God causes everything to work together for the good of those who love God and are called according to his purpose for them.

Romans 8:28, NLT

April 26

Not Sure Yet

In our challenging discussion
I started to tell my college friend
That though I didn't understand electricity
I certainly accepted it.
With an impatient gesture he interrupted me.
"I don't want to hear about electricity.
I just want God."
"How much do you want Him?" I asked.
Nervous silence. Then finally a reply:
"I'm really not sure yet."

Lord, I don't know how long
My seeker-for-God friend
Will continue his flimsy excuses
Or linger in a state of noncommitment
But when he is sure enough to really seek You
He will surely find You.
This is Your personal promise.

Ask and it will be given to you; seek and you will find; knock and
the door will be opened to you. For everyone who asks receives; he
who seeks finds; and to him who knocks, the door will be opened.

Matthew 7:7-8, NIV

April 27

I Trust You

Lord, it was on an April morning

So many years ago

That You said to me so clearly

"Trust Me and you won't be disappointed."

Having heard You on that special morning

I simply cannot "unhear" you now.

I can't forget that morning

Nor do I think You want me to.

Because You live in an eternal Now

Your words are just as relevant today

As they were that long-ago morning.

I *trust* You. You will not disappoint me!

Jesus Christ is the same yesterday and today and forever.

Hebrews 13:8, NIV

April 28

Three Discoveries

I have made three overwhelming discoveries regarding God's
reliable faithfulness:

The first: God will never let us go—*never!* We may fall flat on our
faces. We may resist until we feel exhausted, but *nothing* can
separate us from his matchless love.

The second: God will never let us down—*never!* He is forever
faithful, even when we are faithless. He cannot deny himself.
He will never leave us nor forsake us.

The third: He will never let us off—*never!* Whenever we give in to
temptation, when we determine to have our own way—he says
with all the love of his Father-heart, "I love you too much to
excuse disobedience." Whom he loves, he chastens.

God is determined to bless us. He is eager to show us his
kindness. He is glad to teach us the proper paths; but he *must*
have access to our hearts. He will allow our guilt to become a
burden until conviction comes, then confession, and finally
renewed commitment!

May David's prayer be our prayer:

Teach me to do your will, for you are my God. May your gracious
Spirit lead me forward on a firm footing.   Psalm 143:10, NLT

April 29

Your Child, God

O God
With deep contrition
I shamefully confess
My small concept of You
My puny faith
My limited comprehension.
Forgive me, O God
And enlarge my narrow vision.
Stimulate my trust
As I concentrate on Your greatness.
Give me even now
A true perspective
Of Your majestic power
To totally transform the child
On whom You have set Your love—
The child whose name is engraved
On the palm of Your hand
The child who claims You
As her Maker and Master.
Your child, God!
Me!

Show me the path where I should walk, O Lord; point out the right road for me to follow. Lead me by your truth and teach me, for you are the God who saves me. All day long I put my hope in you.

Psalm 25:4-5, NLT

April 30

How Long Is Everlasting?

O dear God
How long will You ignore me?
How long must I continue to weep before You?
Will You forever keep silent
When I seek Your face?
Surely You know my desperation
And yet I cannot arouse Your attention.
Must I continually stumble
Through dense forests and dark valleys?
Does it matter to You about me?
I don't understand, Lord.
In the past You so lavishly blessed me.
Have I offended You?
Are there false motives that I cannot trace?
Are You searching me out?
O Lord, I cannot endure the thought
That You no longer love me.
Hear my cry, dear God.
Please speak to me.

Listen, dear child
Quietly listen.
I have loved you
With an everlasting love.
How long is everlasting?

But may all who seek you rejoice and be glad in you; may those who love your salvation always say, "The Lord be exalted!" Yet I am poor and needy; may the Lord think of me. You are my help and my deliverer; O my God, do not delay.   Psalm 40:16-17, NIV

May

The Promise of Abundant Life

Lord, you always bring ultimate good

to those who love you. May I never surrender

to the false conclusion that you have no more

for me than what I already have.

You will show me the way of life, granting me the joy of
your presence and the pleasures of living with you forever.
Psalm 16:11, NLT

May 1

Beautiful Belonging

Before I knew You, Lord
It was terribly important
To flaunt my culinary art
With a moist and tender roast.
Now that I'm Yours
It is far more important
To serve Your gentleness
To our guests.

Before I knew You
It was terribly important
To snatch every weed
From our meticulous yard.
Now that I'm Yours
It is far more important

To express neighborly concern
Over the back fence.

Before I knew You
It was terribly important
To check the television schedule
From night to night.
Now that I'm Yours
It is far more important
To check Your plan
From day to day.

What an incredible change—
This Beautiful Belonging!

But the Lord said to her, "My dear Martha, you are so upset over all these details! There is really only one thing worth being concerned about. Mary has discovered it—and I won't take it away from her."

Luke 10:41-42, NLT

May 2

Coincidences

Lord, I was intrigued
With the brilliant vocabulary
Of the patient sitting next to me
In the reception room.
I don't remember
The start of our conversation
But suddenly we were discussing
    prayer.
I shared rather freely
Your pertinent answers
To my day-by-day requests.
Labeling himself a skeptic
He smiled and said courteously
"What you consider answered
    prayer
I choose to call coincidence."
You know how it is with me,
    Lord—

I'm always slightly ill at ease
In the Big Middle
Of a theological discussion.
I'm much more at home in my
    kitchen
Mixing muffin batter
Or tossing green salads.
Frankly I was relieved
When the dentist called my name.
But one thing I do know, Lord
When I pray, "coincidences"
    happen.
When I don't pray they stop . . .

So thank You again and again
For ten thousand "coincidences"
Always in the nick of time
When I pray.

And pray in the Spirit on all occasions with all kinds of prayers and
requests.
Ephesians 6:18, NIV

May 3

Real Problem

Lord

Your dedicated servant said:

"Never doubt in the darkness

What God tells you in the light."

I've got a real problem, Lord.

I doubt even in the light.

Look at the birds. They don't need to plant or harvest or put food
in barns because your heavenly Father feeds them. And you are far
more valuable to him than they are. Can all your worries add a single
moment to your life? Of course not.   Matthew 6:26-27, NLT

May 4

I'm Drowning

Lord, I'm drowning

In a sea of perplexity.

Waves of confusion

Crash over me.

I'm too weak

To shout for help.

Either quiet the waves

Or lift me above them—

It's too late

To learn to swim.

Rise up! Come and help us! Save us because of your unfailing love.

Psalm 44:26, NLT

May 5

Courtesy

I tried to be
Very courteous.
I smiled and said
"No thank You, Lord."
You smiled back and said
"Omit the first word
And I'll be delighted
With your courtesy—
And more delighted
With your trust."
"Thank You, Lord."

Should we accept only good things from the hand of God and never
anything bad?
Job 2:10, NLT

This, Too, Is Faith

Lord, I am desperately afraid

Of tempestuous waves.

Had I been on the ship

The day you stilled the storm

I would have been the first

To scream for help—

This I shamelessly admit.

But, Lord, this too is faith:

Boldly expecting You

To do something about it.

Let us then approach the throne of grace with confidence, so that we may receive mercy and find grace to help us in our time of need.

Hebrews 4:16, NIV

May 7

Once in a While We Can

One bright Sunday when I was twelve, I didn't want to go to church. I wasn't coddling a pent-up rebellion. I simply pictured a leisurely day away from "have to" things.

How to explain and be understood! Finally I just blurted it out as Mother prepared breakfast. She listened attentively.

"Honey," she said calmly, "we can't always do what we feel like doing without hurting someone."

That settled it, I thought. I was sorry I had asked.

Suddenly I heard, "But once in a while we *can* do what we want to—just because we want to. You may stay home this Sunday."

The memory of that day is still vivid. Not because I stayed home from church, but because I learned a profound lesson: *Once in a while we can!*

Once in a while we can get away from alarm clocks, peanut-butter jars, milk cartons . . . away from the shattering pressures of our competitive society.

Once in a while we *need* to get away from work, family, friends, and pressing commitments. Often we lose the capacity for personal enjoyment.

Once in a while we need to walk, think, and meditate. Only God can satisfy our deepest longings. He longs for us to share our private secrets with him.

Once in a while we can.

The Lord is my shepherd; I have everything I need. He lets me rest in green meadows; he leads me beside peaceful streams. He renews my strength. He guides me along right paths, bringing honor to his name.

Psalm 23:1-3, NLT

May 8

Stay There

Lord
Please get me off
This emotional elevator
Which carries me so swiftly
From the basement of despair
To the tenth floor of exhilaration
And down to the basement again.
I'm hoarse from shouting
My fists are blue from pounding
I'm suffocating in this
Dark, windowless box.

Turn and look, dear child.
The door is wide open.
Walk straight into My waiting arms
And stay there.

Come, all you who are thirsty, come to the waters; and you who
have no money, come, buy, and eat! Come, buy wine and milk
without money and without cost. Why spend money on what is not
bread, and you labor on what does not satisfy? Listen, listen to me,
and eat what is good, and your soul will delight with the richest
of fare.   Isaiah 55:1-2, NIV

May 9

Not As They Seem

It would seem, Lord
When You have been our dwelling place
In all generations . . .
When You have guided us
Undergirded us
And enveloped us with love . . .
When You are Bread for the hungry
Rest for the weary
Strength for the powerless
And Joy unspeakable . . .
It would seem, Lord
That we would have more to offer
Than lust
Greed
Hatred
War . . .

But that's precisely why
You came to die:
In the hearts of men
Things are not as they seem.

For God so loved the world that he gave his only Son, so that everyone who believes in him will not perish but have eternal life. God
did not send his Son into the world to condemn it, but to save it.

John 3:16-17, NLT

May 10

Majestic Approval

O God
I'd love to keep
The beauty of this day
Forever and forever:
The sky incredibly blue
New leaves shining
Flowers swaying
In the gentle breeze
Birds with changeful wills
Darting here and there
The lake a sparkling jewel
Surrounded by spicy pines
And You looking down
At Your handiwork
With majestic approval.

The heavens tell of the glory of God. The skies display his marvelous craftsmanship.
Psalm 19:1, NLT

Forgive Me

Lord
So often I am
Fearful
Unbelieving
And apologetic about my faith.
I analyze
Whittle down
And tear apart
Your very words.
I conjure foolish reasons
For my lack of trust
As though You couldn't possibly mean
What You so clearly said.
Yet, all the while You wait for me
To believe *exactly* what You said—
Without exception
Without alteration.
Forgive me for treating You
Like someone who would lie.

God saved you by his special favor when you believed. And you can't
take credit for this; it is a gift from God. Salvation is not a reward
for the good things we have done, so none of us can boast about it.

Ephesians 2:8-9, NLT

May 12

You Did All the Rest

O Lord God!
I did what You asked me to do:
I just opened windows
Wide . . .
Wide . . .
And You did all the rest!
You poured into my heart
A blessed, blissful contentment.
You saturated my mind
With gigantic thoughts of You.
You struck an artesian well within me
Until sheer joy sprang forth.
You led me out of the valley of despair
Into a succession of incredible happenings.
Problems which seemed insurmountable
Melted like wax before my eyes.
Fears faded away like threatening clouds.
You startled me
You amazed me
With the glory of Your revelation.
It is true
Gloriously true—
I have literally walked and breathed with God.
I just opened windows
Wide . . .
Wide . . .
God, You did all the rest!

God is our refuge and strength, an ever-present help in trouble.
Therefore we will not fear, though the earth give way and the
mountains fall into the heart of the sea.   Psalm 46:1-2, NIV

May 13

God's Searchlight

O God
If suddenly You were to reveal
To my family, my friends, my neighbors
Every real thought behind my courteous words
If You were to point to my clenched fist
While my other hand is openly extended
If You were to bring to light
Every masked motive, every selfish act
I would cringe with remorse
And beg You to remove Your light of revelation.
Yet, Lord, when the searchlight of the Holy Spirit
Begins to reveal me to *myself*
I so often close my eyes and turn my back
In a frantic but impossible effort
To escape Your penetrating gaze.
What a staggering contradiction, Lord
What appalling hypocrisy.
Apart from Your grace I am utterly shattered.
I ask You to sweep through me
Purify me, cleanse me completely.
From the depth of my penitent heart
I thank You for Your continual assurance
As I turn toward Your splintered cross:
Because of Your love I *became* Your child
Because of Your grace I *remain* Your child.

"Come now, let us reason together," says the Lord. "Though your
sins be as scarlet, they shall be white as snow; though they are red as
crimson, they shall be like wool."   Isaiah 1:18, NIV

May 14

Motherhood

Motherhood is *now!* The good and the bad of it. The rewards and the trials. Tremendous pressures are placed upon you as a mother, for you have been chosen to work with God in the awesome task of nurturing the priceless treasures God has given you.

As a mother, you accept your children's faltering steps toward independence with discipline, humor, patience, and a tremendous amount of trust. At times the struggles almost become an endurance contest. You wonder if you can handle all the confusion another day: the ringing phone, the broken dishes, the blaring television, the hurtful words. High temperatures, school conferences, dentist appointments, rebellious tears. Is there ever an end?

But suddenly in the midst of turmoil you catch a broad grin. You feel a warm hug. At bedtime somebody prays, "Thank you, God, for Mom and for chocolate-chip cookies . . . and for love."

You renew again your deep desire to create a genuine God-hunger in your children. God has chosen you for such a task as this.

Her children stand and bless her. Her husband praises her: "There are many virtuous and capable women in the world, but you surpass them all!"

Proverbs 31:28-29, NLT

This Beautiful Sunlit Morning

Dear God
On this beautiful sunlit
Morning in May
You've drenched me
With ecstatic joy.
I want to sing and shout
I want to soar with sheer delight.
At the same time I want to sob—
So utterly overwhelmed I am
With the magnitude of You.

O God, I know
I do know
With serene satisfaction
And confident certainty
That I belong to the God
Of the Universe—
To the Creator
Of all that exists.

I do know
That I, a mere mortal
Am forever linked to divine
    destiny—

That my life has purpose and
    dignity.
I do know
That You have chosen me
As the object of Your lavish love
That Your thoughts toward me
Are thoughts of kindness and
    mercy
That You have inscribed me
In the palms of Your hands.

I do know
That all the Love of the Father
And the Life of the Son
And the Power of the Holy Spirit
Are freely, inseparably mine—
Now and through all eternity.
O God
On this beautiful sunlit
Morning in May
I do know.

To our God and Father be glory for ever and ever. Amen.

Philippians 4:20, NIV

May 16

Three Miserable Days

Lord

For three miserable days now

I have stubbornly resisted You.

I've balked and argued

I've looked for possible detours

I've shouted outrageous excuses

And I've tried in every possible way

To sidestep You.

All of this, only to discover

That my clenched-fist resistance

Has been far more unbearable

Than the obedience You required of me.

Lord, may I please have another chance?

When you bow down before the Lord and admit your dependence on
him, he will lift you up and give you honor.   James 4:10, NLT

May 17

Grief

Lord, You who permit my grief
Are the only One
Who can assuage it.
I wonder—
Do you permit grief
That I might learn
To be content
With nothing less
Than the comfort of God?
Whatever the reason
One thing I am learning:
You make useful to me
All that You permit.
So, dear God
Though a great ache
Wells within my heart
I ask You to grip my life.
Empower me to go
From depth to depth with You
Until I am a "wounded healer"
Bringing Your comfort to others
As You are now comforting me.

Even though the fig trees have no blossoms, and there are no grapes on the vine; even though the olive crop fails, and the fields lie empty and barren; even though the flocks die in the fields, and the cattle barns are empty, yet I will rejoice in the Lord! I will be joyful in the God of my salvation. The Sovereign Lord is my strength! He will make me as surefooted as a deer and bring me safely over the mountains.

Habakkuk 3:17-19, NLT

May 18

Forgiving Lord

Forgiving Lord
I long for her release—
My friend who churns
With memories of failure and
    guilt.
She needs to feel sure and serene
Knowing You are holding her
    fast.
She needs to understand
That her continual remorse
Is a sheer waste of energy and
    time.
In no way can she change the past
Or relive it
Or rectify it.
Lord, she is torturing herself
In her circle of regret.

Please speak to her, God.
May she no longer censure herself
For what once happened.
Rather, direct her attention
To what is happening now.
May she stop berating herself
For her mismanaged past.
Empower her to concentrate
On managing the present.
Heal her, Lord!
She is so occupied
With morbid introspection.
Give her a fresh, breathtaking
    glimpse
Of the joy that can be hers
When she is totally occupied with
    You.

I lift up my eyes to the hills—where does my help come from?
My help comes from the Lord, the Maker of heaven and earth.

Psalm 121:1-2, NIV

New-born Ecstasy

When I resolve to come to You
Amid the chunks and cracks
Of all my mundane days—
When I resolve to listen
Really listen to Your gentle voice
Suddenly I know anew
That You are life
And life is joy!
Like a singing brook
Joy splashes over
All the common "dailies"
Until each empty space
Of my hungry heart
Is touched with new-born ecstasy.

Shout with joy to the Lord, O earth! Worship the Lord with gladness. Come before him, singing with joy. Acknowledge that the Lord is God! He made us, and we are his. We are his people, the sheep of his pasture.

Psalm 100:1-3, NLT

All

O God

Thank You, thank You

For Your reiterated ALL. . . .

You have promised:

ALL my needs shall be supplied.

ALL grace shall abound toward me.

ALL the promises are mine.

ALL things asked I shall receive.

ALL sufficiency for ALL things.

You are with me always

ALL the days.

And today!

Give thanks to the Lord, for he is good!   Psalm 136:1, NLT

Total Abandonment

With deep conviction I know I must habitually put to death every thought and every action that brings displeasure to God. I must daily come to grips with what my self demands. I must give up, and then give over every part of me that spells my name. Only then can I truly experience a radical soul release—which I need above all else.

When sin is continually indulged, it grows. At times slowly, but always surely. A gradual decline becomes obvious. Agony of soul begins to consume a previous longing for God. My hardened heart seeks every possible way to justify itself. An irrational dislike of others captures my distraught emotions. Distrust fosters bitterness. Finally life becomes empty, barren, dismal.

I genuinely thank God for letting me become so miserable with life that only one thing matters: Total abandonment to him, who calls me to himself. How relieving and releasing it is to recapture a renewed hunger and thirst for him, the true and living God. He alone is my heart's desire.

If you search for [the Lord] with all your heart and soul, you will find him.
Deuteronomy 4:29, NLT

Fed Up

Lord, I'm utterly fed up

With my foolish and futile attempt

To live a facsimile of genuine Christianity.

Like thousands of jagged Christians

I am just so "sick and tired

Of being sick and tired."

I want to withdraw my membership

From the Society of Self-Improvement

With its heavy dues and dismal news.

With all my breathless effort

I am no further improved

Than the day I joined.

So please take me as I am

And make me what I could never be

Apart from You: transparently real!

But now God has shown us a different way of being right in his
sight—not by obeying the law but by the way promised in the
Scriptures long ago. We are made right in God's sight when we
trust in Jesus Christ to take away our sins. And we all can be
saved in this same way, no matter who we are or what we have done.

Romans 3:21-22, NLT

May 23

Intimate Closeness

You promise, dear God

That when I draw close to You

You will draw close to me.

Lord, I give myself to You unreservedly.

Teach me more and more

Of intimate closeness

And fill my heart with You alone.

To walk arm-in-arm with You

Down every winding path

Seems to me

The dearest of all delights.

May 24

Freedom

For so long, dear God

I stared with dreadful fascination

At the thick, heavy chains

Binding my burdened life

When all the while You were waiting

For my personal consent

To break the chains and set me free.

Oh, what liberating joy

When I finally said Yes!

Oh, what a miserable person I am! Who will free me from this life
that is dominated by sin? Thank God! The answer is in Jesus Christ
our Lord.   Romans 7:24-25, NLT

May 25

Never Too Late

Sometimes, dear Lord
You work so slowly!

Tell Me, dear child
Have I ever been too late?

Oh, the depth of the riches of the wisdom and knowledge of God!
How unsearchable his judgments, and his paths beyond tracing out!

Romans 11:33, NIV

May 26

Very Different

Lord

Please put me

Where the talents and gifts

You've given me

Can be best used.

Put me, I pray

Where I can best serve You.

This is the deep longing

Of my heart.

My child

I will put you

Where you can best glorify Me.

This may be very different

Than all your present dreams.

Who is able to advise the Spirit of the Lord? Who knows enough
to be his teacher or counselor?
                                                    Isaiah 40:13, NLT

May 27

One Stupendous Thing

O dear God

If You love me at all

(And I want to believe You do)

I beg You to do one stupendous thing

For my torn and bleeding heart:

Please dear Lord

Take the place

Of what You've taken away.

I cannot survive

I cannot endure

Unless You grant this request.

And this same God who takes care of me will supply all your needs from his glorious riches, which have been given to us in Christ Jesus.

Philippians 4:19, NLT

May 28

One Early Evening

One early evening I knelt in the peaceful quiet of our blue-and-white bedroom and asked the Holy Spirit to permeate my life. My words were simple but honest: "Make me a woman after God's own heart."

I don't know what I expected exactly. Waves of ecstasy? Easter bells? A dramatic transformation? None of these things happened. I still washed dishes, baked cookies, washed clothes, and answered the phone in the same methodical way. When I grocery shopped, the money didn't miraculously stretch. When I stood on the scale I wasn't five pounds lighter.

But gradually, ever so gradually, as I trusted God's plan in fulfilling my request, I discovered old fears were disintegrating. A new confidence in God was emerging. I was less insistent about having my own way. Best of all, God's Word was becoming more *alive* as I read day after day.

I'm sure it's but the beginning. I have asked God to do whatever he needs to do to make me all he wants me to be. His promise captures my waiting heart:

For God is working in you, giving you the desire to obey him and the power to do what pleases him.   Philippians 2:13, NLT

I Dare to Believe

"Out of the depths I cry to You,
O Lord."
On this day of remorse and
turmoil
The Psalmist's cry is my cry.
Trembling, crumbling, out of the
depths I cry.
And yet, in the throes of my
anguish, O God
I dare to believe
You see my groping and grasping.
You hear my sighs and sobs.
I dare to believe
You can break through the
emotional blockades
You can rebuild my broken
dreams.
Though my words seem drenched
with presumption
To those who march with illusive
courage
I dare to believe

Your love is unquenchable
Your faithfulness is inexhaustible.
I dare to believe
You delight to draw me to
Yourself
You long to silence my desperate
cry.
I dare to believe
I will yet hear Your gentle words
"I am your Father.
Come home."

Weeping child
It is true
That I am your Father.
Now dare to believe
You are home.

Humble yourselves, therefore, under God's mighty hand, that he may
lift you up in due time. Cast all your anxiety on him because he cares
for you.
1 Peter 5:6-7, NIV

Two Questions

O God

In my fear and frenzy

In my darkness and dread

My screaming question is

"Where *are* You?"

Wandering child

When things were going well

And you carelessly ignored Me

Where were you?

God has said, "I will never fail you. I will never forsake you."

Hebrews 13:5, NLT

May 31

I Can Settle for That

The word *rebellion* frightens me.
I always associate it with
Revolt . . . terrorism . . . riots . . .
    death . . .
With economic and social
    issues . . .
With the drug scene
That promotes life without
    purpose.
I associate it with tempestuous
    waves of change
That leap up like wild animals.
Like the disciples in the storm
I want to awaken You, Lord.
I wonder why You seem to be
    sleeping.

But, Lord, maybe I don't
Really know You very well.
Maybe I don't let God be God.
After all, *You* are not frightened.
You do not hold Your hands up
    in despair.
You never say, "You should have
    come yesterday."

Nor do You say, "You're the
    wrong age and color."
You never say, "You're too timid,
    too slow."

You simply tell me to step out
Of my rocking boat.
You tell me to walk the waves with
    You.
You assure me You are not asleep.
You tell me to show genuine love
To a desperately needy world.

You insist it is far better
To walk over the billows than to go
    under them.
You tell me if I die in the attempt
At least I will die victoriously.
Then, facing me directly, You ask
"Can You settle for that?"
Lord, if You are with me
I can settle for that!

And so, dear brothers and sisters, I plead with you to give your bodies to God. Let them be a living and holy sacrifice—the kind he will accept. When you think of what he has done for you, is this too much to ask?

Romans 12:1, NLT

June

The Promise of Being Known

Though there is much about life that disturbs

and puzzles us, there is one satisfying consolation:

We know that God knows! And he can be trusted!

Trust in the Lord with all your heart; do not depend on
your own understanding. Seek his will in all you do, and
he will direct your paths.   Proverbs 3:5-6, NLT

You're in My Way

This morning, Lord
I heard a distraught mother
Say to her lively son
"You're in my way—move."
This very same morning
You said to me
"You're in My way—stay."
How good it is
To be Your child.

June 2

When I Am with You

When I am with You, Lord
It is as though
I were given
A cup of cool water
Dipped from
An ever-flowing
Never-ceasing stream.
The water glistens
As a piece of clear ice
Tingles against
The side of my cup.
I want to drink
More
And more
And more
As though I could
Never drink enough—
And yet while I drink
I am satisfied
Completely.

What a strange and beautiful
Paradox!

Whoever drinks the water I give him will never thirst. Indeed, the
water I give him will become in him a spring of water welling up to
eternal life.
John 4:14, NIV

June 3

Painful

Lord

Too often my talents

Have been on display

For public inspection.

Now I am painfully learning

The only important thing:

Your reflection.

Who is Apollos, and who is Paul, that we should be the cause of
such quarrels? Why, we're only servants. Through us God caused
you to believe. Each of us did the work the Lord gave us.

1 Corinthians 3:5, NLT

June 4

Mountains——Molehills

Oh, Lord

You've done it again

You've turned

My flimsy little tune

Into a swelling crescendo.

But that's the way You are—

Always making mountains

Out of our molehills of joy.

June 5

Resemblance

Lord, somewhere I read

That when two people

Love deeply

When they live together

Sharing

Caring

Giving

Forgiving

Eventually they begin

To resemble each other.

Lord, how long will it be

Before I look like *You?*

And we, who with unveiled faces all reflect the Lord's glory, are being transformed into his likeness with ever-increasing glory, which comes from the Lord, who is the Spirit. 2 Corinthians 3:18, NIV

June 6

Take Over

At first, Lord, I asked You
To take sides with me.
With David the Psalmist
I circled and underlined:
"The Lord is for me . . ."
"Maintain my rights, O Lord . . ."
"Let me stand above my foes . . ."
But with all my pleading
I lay drenched in darkness
Until in utter confusion I cried
"Don't take sides, Lord
Just take over."
And suddenly it was morning.

Teach me to do your will, for you are my God. May your gracious
Spirit lead me forward on a firm footing.   Psalm 143:10, NLT

June 7

A Friendship Observed

After my father's death, I sat in his quiet office sorting through
years of sermons and journals. A few tears fell on the pages.
My task was very personal. Hundreds of memories encircled
the room.

I was amazed, yet pleased, when I began to compare my
journals with my father's. Our groping and intense struggles,
our affirmations and confessions were so often interlaced. It
would never have occurred to us to share our journals while
Dad was living. Diaries, letters, journals, and even phone calls
were private.

Today I reflect upon my own record of life—page after page
of spiritual encounters. Anguish, questions, purging, joy,
discipline, insights, ecstasy, faith—*God's whispered secrets.*

Suddenly the early beginning became very much alive: A
little girl, seven or eight, hearing her father say, "If you'll
listen—really listen—God will whisper secrets to you!"

My father had said something very beautiful and strange.
How did he know that God would whisper secrets to *me?*

But as I sorted through my father's careful recounting of his
inner life and journey, it suddenly became very clear: *He, too, had
heard God's secrets!*

"I know the plans I have for you," says the Lord. "They are plans for
good and not for disaster, to give you a future and a hope. In those days
when you pray, I will listen. If you look for me in earnest, you will
find me when you seek me."   Jeremiah 29:11-13, NLT

A Better Way

A thousand times, dear Lord

In moments of fierce temptation

I have asked You to help me.

But at last I have learned a better way:

I no longer ask merely for help

I look up into Your gentle face

And ask You to do it all.

As a father has compassion on his children, so the Lord has
compassion on those who fear him; for he knows how we are
formed, he remembers that we are dust.   Psalm 103:13-14, NIV

June 9

Rare Moments of Delight

Because You are God
And Your Word is unquestionable
There are things I assuredly know
Even when my heart is a brambled desert
And every ounce of emotion is drained:
I know Your love is everlasting
I know You will never forsake me
Nor will you leave me comfortless
I know I may come to you boldly
I know you will teach and instruct me
You will guide me with Your eye
I know my past is forgiven
And my future is secure.
But oh, dear God
How I praise You for the marvel
Of those rare, mysterious moments
When suddenly, without a flash or a sound
You add to my *knowing*
The ecstasy of *feeling*
And I am lifted to peaks of delight!

Be exalted, O God, above the highest heavens. May your glory shine
over all the earth.   Psalm 108:5, NLT

June 10

I Know Who I Am

There he sat on his front porch
(Probably three or four years old)
And when he flashed a merry smile
I stopped to ask his name.
"I'm my daddy's boy," he said, grinning
And then he was off to play.
I still don't know his name, Lord
But it doesn't matter.
He knows who he is
And that makes everything all right.

Thank You, Lord
With all my heart
That I may say with genuine confidence
"I'm my Father's child."
That makes everything all right.

So you should not be like cowering, fearful slaves. You should behave instead like God's very own children, adopted into his family—calling him "Father, dear Father." For his Holy Spirit speaks to us deep in our hearts and tells us that we are God's children.   Romans 8:15-16, NLT

June 11

Solution

Today, after hours of praying

For something that didn't come

Something I so desperately craved

I see anew, dear God

That with all my clamoring

And agonized pleading

I simply cannot change You.

No, dear child

But I can change you.

I the Lord do not change.   Malachi 3:6, NIV

June 12

Overwhelmed

All day long, dear God

I have been overwhelmed

With my failure

And folly.

Now please overwhelm me

With Your faithfulness

And forgiveness.

Lord, if you kept a record of our sins, who, O Lord, could ever survive? But you offer forgiveness, that we might learn to fear you.

Psalm 130:3-4, NLT

June 13

Try Me

O Lord

Is there anyone

In all the world

Who really understands me?

Yes, dear child

Me.

O Lord, you have searched me and you know me. You know when
I sit and when I rise; you perceive my thoughts from afar.

Psalm 139:1-2, NIV

June 14

Welcome Home

I remember so well the long-ago day when my brother of seven years wrote a note to my parents. He was anything but happy. So many alibis, so many collisions with trouble!

There had been an accumulation of things: He hadn't picked up his clothes. He's tracked mud on the carpeting. He had pinched his best friend to see how loud he would scream. One by one his privileges were taken away—so he wrote: *I'm running away. P.S. If I get hungry maybe I'll come back someday.*

"Someday" didn't take long. After an hour or so the young prodigal came home. He was penitent and hungry. There were tears and hugs. There was forgiveness. He was home!

So often I too run away: when prayers are unanswered . . . when God says no and I want him to say yes . . . when I want to go one way and he points to another.

Yet when I run from God I feel desolate, lonely. I hunger for his presence. When I finally begin the long walk home, he is waiting. With arms wide open he welcomes me. He forgives me. I discover again, there's no place like home!

Come, let us return to the Lord. Hosea 6:1, NLT

June 15

Which, Lord?

Lord

I always seem to be

The child in Your family

Who needs the most chastening.

Is it because

I'm so unmanageable

Or is it because

You love me so much?

My child, don't ignore it when the Lord disciplines you, and don't be discouraged when he corrects you. For the Lord corrects those he loves, just as a father corrects a child in whom he delights.

Proverbs 3:11-12, NLT

June 16

Increase My Enthusiasm

Lord, with gratitude

And genuine enthusiasm

I pray for those who love me.

But I must ask You now

To increase my enthusiasm

As I pray for those who don't.

Bless those who persecute you; bless and do not curse.

Romans 12:14, NIV

Intimacy

Dear God

May I live intimately close to You

Above the perplexities of Life

With the moon under my feet!

At the same time, God

Humble me, gentle me

Create in me a deepening awareness

So that I shall never miss

A cushion of violets hiding in the sod

Or the cry of a frightened child

Or the desperate sob of a lonely heart.

"'You must love the Lord your God with all your heart, all your soul, all your mind, and all your strength.' The second is equally important: 'Love your neighbor as yourself.' No other commandment is greater than these."

Mark 12:30-31, NLT

June 18

A Doubt

Sometimes, dear Lord
You don't seem
To love me at all.

Sometimes, dear child
You seem to ignore
The eternal facts.

He passed in front of Moses and said, "I am the Lord, I am the
Lord, the merciful and gracious God. I am slow to anger and rich
in unfailing love and faithfulness."

Exodus 34:6, NLT

The Prayer

For so many anguished months
I've been waiting for You to
 answer
The one longing desire of my
 heart.
I've begged, pleaded, agonized.
I've prayed at times fumblingly
At other times intensely.
I've knelt and prayed.
I've buried my head in my pillow
 and prayed.
I've prayed before breakfast
And after lunch.
I've prayed before dawn
And after dark.
I've prayed with spontaneous
 outbursts
While tears washed my face.
I've prayed over our kitchen sink

And as I shopped for groceries.
I've prayed amid screeching traffic.
At times I've prayed with
 confidence
At other times with fear.
And yet, Lord, though I have
 waited
Though I have strained to listen
There is no answer.
I hear nothing . . . just nothing.
O God, I am so puzzled, so
 bewildered.
A frightening thought haunts me.
Could it be true, Lord?
Don't You love me anymore?
My child
Because I love you so much
I wait for you to let Me
Remove the harmful desire.

Wait patiently for the Lord. Be brave and courageous. Yes, wait patiently for the Lord.

Psalm 27:14, NLT

June 20

New Beginning

O God

What shall I do?

I am at the total end

Of myself.

Wonderful, dear child!

Now start your new beginning

With Me.

He who was seated on the throne said, "I am making everything new!"

Revelation 21:5, NIV

June 21

A Woman Who Is Real

A woman who is real knows that in her family she must sometimes back off so God can move in.

A woman who is real continually builds a monument of healthy memories for her family. She believes that memories create security and establish values. Above all, they record a growing history of God's unwavering faithfulness.

A woman who is real refuses to let her life be cluttered with unconfessed guilts. She guards her tongue, knowing how quickly a little spark can ignite a huge fire.

A woman who is real listens well. She is careful not to break into an ongoing conversation to tell her own story.

A woman who is real sheds the masks of pretense. There are no dark corners in her heart—no credibility gap between who she is and how she accepts others.

A woman who is real feels no need to "prove" her Christianity; she herself is walking proof.

She is clothed with strength and dignity, and she laughs with no fear of the future. When she speaks, her words are wise, and kindness is the rule when she gives instructions. . . . Charm is deceptive, and beauty does not last; but a woman who fears the Lord will be greatly praised. Reward her for all she has done. Let her deeds publicly declare her praise.
Proverbs 31:25-31, NLT

June 22

The Living God

I place my whole confidence

In the Living God.

Not because things

Are going my way.

Not because I have what I want.

Not because I understand

All the inexplainables

Or because I am immune

To problems and pain and sorrow.

But despite my questions

My reversals, my disappointments

Despite my sorrow and tears

I place my whole confidence

In the Living God

For He alone can see me through.

He alone is worthy of my trust.

Whom have I in heaven but you? And earth has nothing I desire
besides you. My flesh and my heart may fail, but God is the strength
of my heart and my portion forever.　　　Psalm 73:25-26, NIV

June 23

Always There

So often, Lord

I reach the bottom of the abyss.

So often I taste the dregs

Of my own helplessness.

Yet it is there, *exactly there*

That You come to my immediate rescue.

When I feel totally impoverished

Of all self-sufficiency

When I want to vanish into nowhere

From the depths of despair

I call Your name

And You are always there for me!

The Lord will guide you always; he will satisfy your needs in a sun-scorched land and will strengthen your frame. You will be like a well-watered garden, like a spring whose waters never fail.

Isaiah 58:11, NIV

June 24

Irreversible Yes

God, You have done

A beautiful thing for me.

You have freed me from the dissatisfaction

Of so many empty days and months.

Into my impoverished heart

You have poured life-changing thoughts of You

Making each new day gloriously rich.

You have struck a deep artesian well in my soul

As sheer joy springs forth.

All because in an act of honest surrender

When life had lost its challenge

I said an irreversible YES to You!

I am the bread of life.   John 6:48, NIV

June 25

Life's Whys

Lord

If You were to answer

All of life's whys

Surely You would have started

With Your servant Job.

Instead, Your determined goal for Job

Was unrivaled loyalty and trust.

And so, dear God

As achingly difficult as it often is

Enable me to trust You

With such total abandonment

That You will hear no complaining

When I hear no explaining.

Blessed rather are those who hear the word of God and obey it.

Luke 11:28, NIV

Divided Heart

Lord
I am so often tormented
By my lack of clear direction—
So often disturbed
By my divided heart.

I am like a little child
Who wants to rock her doll
And jump rope at the same time.
I want to obey You in part
If I can choose the areas of
    obedience.
I want to be real except at those
    moments
When compromise is more
    appealing.
I want to be half-motivated
And half-satisfied with things as
    they are.

I want to walk a straight path
If now and then I can enjoy
A few side trips into the far
    country.
I don't want to be a miserable
    sinner
But neither do I feel excited
About being a stoic saint.
I want to be partly Yours
And partly my own.

But in the secret chamber
Of my divided heart
I am so often disquieted
By the pointed question:
"Why do you so foolishly
Mix weeds with seeds?"

Stop loving this evil world and all that it offers you, for when you love the world, you show that you do not have the love of the Father in you.

1 John 2:15, NLT

June 27

Soul Struggle

Her uncontrollable sobs know no respite.
"What is wrong with me"
She stammers convulsively
"That love has passed me by?
Am I so ugly, so stupidly plain?
Am I some kind of an oddity?
Doesn't God love me anymore?"

Lord, there are times when she hides
Behind a sophisticated facade
But today she is not pretending.
In her deep loneliness
There are no words to comfort her.
You alone can release her
From her shadowy world.
You alone can break the bleakness
And produce the firm conviction
Of Your measureless love.
Lord, my part in her soul's struggle
Is to reach for her hand.
Your part is to reach for her heart.

He tends his flock like a shepherd; He gathers the lambs in his arms
and carries them close to his heart.
Isaiah 40:11, NIV

June 28

Listening Love

Listening love is one of the greatest gifts we can give our mates, our families, and our friends. Too often we settle for surface talk or icy silences, for monologues or cutoffs, for defenses. What a difference when we follow the principles of listening love!

Listening love is courteous. It says . . .
   I will strive not to interrupt or outguess you. I will not finish your sentences or break into your thoughts.

Listening love is attentive. It says . . .
   I will give you my undivided attention. I will not turn you off or leave you isolated.

Listening love is patient. It says . . .
   I will not rush you or insist on a right-now conclusion.

Listening love is kind. It says . . .
   I will not shame you with sarcastic retorts. I will not belittle you.

Listening love is objective. It says . . .
   I will try to be informative rather than opinionated. I will not attempt to think for you.

Listening love is unselfish. It says . . .
   I will guard against overconfidence and trite "spiritual" answers.

Listening love is prayerful. It says . . .
   I will pray for insight, for wisdom, and for gentle reactions.

May the words of my mouth and the meditation of my heart be pleasing in your sight, O Lord, my Rock and my Redeemer.

Psalm 19:14, NIV

June 29

Live by the Moment

O Lord
I am staggered by the enormity
Of the countless tasks
Flung at me today.
I simply don't know
How to tackle them all.
What shall I do first, Lord?
How shall I make room
For the interruptions
That are bound to come?
What shall I leave undone
When interruptions take priority?
Your Word clearly states
That You will guide me
With Your counsel.
You have promised Your wisdom
When my lack is so great.
I dare not plunge into the day
Without seeking Your guidance.
Lord, will You help me?

Anxious child
Live today
By the moment
Not by the year.

In repentance and rest is your salvation, in quietness and trust is your
strength.
                                                            Isaiah 30:15, NIV

June 30

I Wait for You

O God

I have waited so long

Under dark clouds of trial and testing

And yet Your promise is clear and precise:

"Blessed are all those that wait for Him."

Though I see no glimmer of hope

Though my tears come unbidden

I am still waiting

For the clouds of trial

To break into refreshing showers of blessing.

Because You have promised, dear Lord

Surely my waiting cannot be in vain.

I wait for You . . . I wait for You . . . I wait.

But the Lord still waits for you to come to him so he can show you his love and compassion. For the Lord is a faithful God. Blessed are those who wait for him to help them.   Isaiah 30:18, NLT

July

The Promise of Faithfulness

Lord, you assure me of two things:

You are God, and you are good.

God, who began the good work within you, will continue
his work until it is finally finished.   Philippians 1:6, NLT

July 1

The Task

Lord, You give me a task
So utterly impossible
So totally beyond comprehension—
The very thought of it
Startles me.
I want to run hide escape
Anything, Lord.

Then You electrify me
You invade and permeate me
You penetrate every fiber of me
Until the task is accomplished
By Your own magnificent power.

Then You praise the performance
Your creativity achieved
And You reward me beyond expectation—
As though I had done it
All by myself.
My Father.

"Not by might nor by power, but by my Spirit", says the Lord
Almighty.   Zechariah 4:6, NIV

Illusive Dreams

Sometimes, Lord
I think I spend my entire life
Working toward illusive dreams.
I dream that someday things will be
Exactly as I want them:
I'll ride on the crest
Of my noble achievements.
With an easygoing independence
I'll keep my confident cool
My house will stay spotless
My budget will balance
My family will applaud me
My friends will acclaim me
I'll glow with charisma.
Lord, am I missing the mark?
Is there a chance for my dreams?

Child of My Plan
Seek first the Kingdom of God
And His righteousness
And every plan of Mine
Will exceed by far
All your illusive dreams.

But seek first his kingdom and his righteousness, and all these things
will be given to you as well.   Matthew 6:33, NIV

July 3

You Are Free

O God
I read today
That the sons of Jacob
And their descendants
Had lived in Egypt 430 years.
But on the last day
Of the 430th year
Your people left Egypt
And the cruel bondage
They had painfully endured.
This was the time You selected.
God, what time have You selected
To free me from the cruel tyranny
That binds me without mercy to myself?

Chosen child
In My Son
You are even now
Completely free.
Accept your freedom!
Walk out this very moment
Into the radiant company
Of My people.

So now there is no condemnation for those who belong to Christ Jesus. For the power of the life-giving Spirit has freed you through Christ Jesus from the power of sin that leads to death.

Romans 8:1-2, NLT

July 4

Fourth of July

I was thinking, Lord—
Our Fourth of July pattern
Seldom varies;
Hot humid air
Hamburger fry
Tender corn
Fresh strawberry ice cream
Then finally
Those traditional sparklers
When darkness tiptoes in.

Funny thing about sparklers—
We never tire of their
Noiseless beauty . . .
Lord, now that I have signed
My Declaration of Dependence
Make me Your sparkler
Noiseless
But beautiful
Especially in the dark.

You are the light of the world—like a city on a mountain, glowing in
the night for all to see. Don't hide your light under a basket! Instead,
put it on a stand and let it shine for all. In the same way, let your
good deeds shine out for all to see, so that everyone will praise your
heavenly Father.   Matthew 5:14-16, NLT

July 5

The Facts

Lord

When I feel I can't possibly make it

When I feel deluged with problems

When I feel helpless

Against the strange twistings of life

When I feel there is no way out

The FACT is

You have a Plan

You know what You're about.

The FACT is

The greater the strategy of the Enemy

The greater the assurance of victory.

The FACT is

The worst may seem to happen

But the best is on the way.

God, hold me to the facts.

Your word, O Lord, is eternal; it stands firm in the heavens. Your
faithfulness continues through all generations; you established the
earth, and it endures.   Psalm 119:89-90, NIV

July 6

Joy

Joy!

My favorite word.

Circumstances may determine my happiness

But, Lord, You determine my joy.

Joy is sweetly honest.

No wonder the minister said:

"You can't hide joy if you have it—

You can't fake it if you don't."

Who can manufacture it, Lord?

Joy is Your creation.

Who may have it?

Anyone who asks.

Thank You, Lord

For joy!

Don't be dejected and sad, for the joy of the Lord is your strength!
Nehemiah 8:10, NLT

July 7

It Takes a Lifetime

How I love the words of the apostle Paul.

"I don't mean to say . . . that I have already reached perfection! But I keep working toward that day when I will finally be all that Christ Jesus saved me for and wants me to be. No, dear brothers and sisters, I am still not all I should be, but I am focusing all my energies on this one thing: Forgetting the past and looking forward to what lies ahead, I strain to reach the end of the race and receive the prize for which God, through Christ Jesus, is calling us up to heaven" Philippians 3:12-14, NLT.

What tremendous encouragement! Paul, who knew Jesus Christ so intimately, whose consuming desire was to please him, who endured illness, imprisonment, shipwreck, beatings, mockery, and heartache all for the sake of Christ—this very same Paul confessed he hadn't "arrived." God was still growing him!

I see again, while my conversion took but a moment, my growth takes an entire lifetime. In God's great wisdom and knowledge he anticipates the finished product while he lovingly takes me through the long, long process.

July 8

Destined

God, I am destined for You!

I was created for You!

Nothing I can ever do or think or feel

Can be separated from You.

With all my inner struggles

My self-absorption

My lethargy and fraud

I cannot alter to one degree

Your settled intention

Your divine purpose:

I was made to bring glory to You!

Long ago, even before he made the world, God loved us and chose us in Christ to be holy and without fault in his eyes. His unchanging plan has always been to adopt us into his own family by bringing us to himself through Jesus Christ. And this gave him great pleasure.

Ephesians 1:4-5, NLT

July 9

Finally—Immediately

Lord

You said so gently

So persistently

"Give Me your weariness

And I'll give you My rest."

I did—finally.

You did—immediately.

Then, Lord, I marveled

That I had waited so long.

Then Jesus said, "Come to me, all of you who are weary and carry heavy burdens, and I will give you rest." Matthew 11:28, NLT

July 10

Rivers and Rivers

O my Father
My heart longs for You!
Fill me to capacity with Your Spirit . . .
No, Father, I'm sorry—
That's not sufficient.
Fill me to *overflowing* with Your Spirit
And then increase my capacity
That there might be still more overflow.
Out of my life
May there flow rivers
And rivers
And still more rivers
Of Living Water
Bringing relief, release
And exhilarating refreshment
To a bruised and broken world
Where thirst can never be quenched
Apart from You.

If anyone is thirsty, let him come to me and drink. Whoever believes
in me, as the Scripture has said, streams of living water will flow from
within him.   John 7:37-38, NIV

July 11

He Can Be Trusted

If You, dear God

Could entrust

To Jesus, Your Son

The salvation of the world

Throughout all eternity

Then surely I can entrust

To Jesus, my Savior

The solution to my problem

Today.

Give your burdens to the Lord, and he will take care of you. He will not permit the godly to slip and fall. Psalm 55:22, NLT

July 12

I Trust You

O God, I trust You.
I don't understand
I cannot begin to comprehend
The wisdom of Your way
In my torn and tangled life
But I am steadfastly believing
That Your plan for me today
Must be—
Surely it *must* be
As kind
As loving
As profitable
As Your plan for me
In joyful days now past.
You are the same
Yesterday
And today
And forever
So, dear God
I trust You.

Jesus Christ is the same yesterday and today and forever.

Hebrews 13:8, NIV

July 13

Don't You Understand?

But Lord

Don't You understand?

If I can't, I can't!

But child

Don't you understand?

If I can, I can!

Things which are

Impossible with you

Are possible with Me.

For nothing is impossible with God.   Luke 1:37, NLT

July 14

A Family Pledge

- We will permit God to use our conflicts and mixed emotions as lessons in quiet growth. With loving patience, without ridicule or judgment, we will support each other in the gradual untangling of built-in defenses.
- We will focus on each other as persons made in the image of God. We will seek to please rather than to pressure, to delight rather than to demand, to give rather than to get.
- We will share the humdrums as well as the highlights, the tears as well as the laughter, the defeats as well as the victories.
- We will not insist on perfection—rather we will anticipate growth. We will not compete for the mountaintop, rather we will climb the mountain together. We will wait for each other if one of us gets behind.
- We will lift our hearts in a celebration of gratitude for God's amazing love, which makes our family love possible.
- We will love each other as we do these things.

Anyone who listens to my teaching and obeys me is wise, like a person who builds a house on solid rock. Matthew 7:24, NLT

July 15

Until She Is Willing

Please, dear God
Assure her of my loving concern.
Help her to know I care for her
And genuinely long to befriend
    her
But she is so frantically fretful
So steeped in self-pity
That any suggestion I casually make
Seems only to flame her hostility.

God, I want to understand her
    limitations.
Guard me against being cheaply
    cheerful.
I'll walk with her eagerly toward
    health
No matter how steep the climb
Or how prolonged the effort.

I'll listen to her, pray with her
But until she is willing to change
I can no longer be her crutch.
She grasps so intensely
I sometimes feel strangled.
The more heavily she leans
The more locked-in she becomes.

Lord, I know only one thing to do:
I release her completely to You.
Speak to her festering heart
Find *some* way of letting her know
That You alone are her Answer—
You have no competitor.
Show her, dear God
That she'll never be free to step
    out
Until she asks You to step in.

". . . Apart from me you can do nothing." John 15:5, NIV

July 16

What's Myself Doing to Myself?

With childish intensity she asked
"What's myself doing to myself?"
I couldn't help but smile
As she stood before the mirror
Struggling so impatiently
With a stubborn jacket zipper.

But I'm not smiling now, Lord
As I pass my own mirror
And glance at the tension
Etching my somber face.
I'm frightened, Lord.
Her innocent question clutches
    me:
"What's myself doing to myself?"

Frustrated, frantic
So often breathless
Too many irons in the fire . . .
What am I doing to my body—
To my mind, my emotions?

What am I doing to my family?
What am I doing to Your Plan
For my personal fulfillment?
Why do I live like this, Lord
As though Your world
Couldn't exist without me?
Why do I so often
Tear myself from Your control?

Dear Lord, calm me.
Pull me off the merry-go-round
Of converging conflicts.
Give balance to my boggled mind.
This very hour, Lord
Infuse me with Your poise and
    power
Until my total self
Is submerged in You—Yourself.
Only then will I be free
To be myself.

Don't worry about anything; instead, pray about everything. Tell God what you need, and thank him for all he has done. If you do this, you will experience God's peace, which is far more wonderful than the human mind can understand. His peace will guard your hearts and minds as you live in Christ Jesus.   Philippians 4:6-7, NLT

July 17

Intrusions

A thousand intrusions
Have crowded in on my life today.
My reaction, Lord?
I've resented every one.
And now I read in Your Word
That I'm to put out the welcome sign!
In fact, I must welcome each intrusion
As a personal friend.
(Perhaps even serve tea, Lord?)
You assure me that You have a purpose
For their continual persistence:
My faith needs depth
My endurance needs development.

I have no argument with that, Lord
But I had hoped that an hour or two
Of trial and testing would suffice.
Or a day at most, dear God.
But again You remind me
That the process must continue
Until maturity becomes my password
And independence becomes my goal
And the Crown of Life becomes my reward.

No discipline is enjoyable while it is happening—it is painful! But afterward there will be a quiet harvest of right living for those who are trained in this way.

Hebrews 12:11, NLT

July 18

Green Light

Thank You, dear Lord

That I need never

Push through jumbled traffic

Or maneuver around sudden detours

To get to Your Throne Room.

All the signal lights are green.

So let us come boldly to the throne of our gracious God. There we will receive his mercy, and we will find grace to help us when we need it.
Hebrews 4:16, NLT

July 19

The Next Thing

O Lord
I love what You said to me
In Your Word today:
"In the place
Where you have walked in defeat
There will I cause victory
To break forth."

Father, I look to You
To do that very thing.
You will not let me
Be ultimately defeated.
And when the battle is won
I must confidently ask
What is the next thing?

He holds victory in store for the upright, he is a shield to those whose
walk is blameless, for he guards the course of the just and protects the
way of his faithful ones.

Proverbs 2:7-8, NIV

July 20

A Quiet Tongue

Lord, a revealing fact
Began to surface today:
I talk more than I listen.
I seem to be thoroughly convinced
That my ideas
My inspiring experiences
My bits of wisdom
Are exactly what all my friends
    need.
Too often I break into
    conversations
Confident that my enlightened
    insight
Will solve the predicament—
Whatever it is.
Obviously, I feel more
    comfortable
When I'm expounding.

But this morning at a Bible study
I cringed when I read Your
    command
In the first chapter of James:

"Don't ever forget
That it is best to listen much
Speak little, and not become
    angry."
At first I wanted to run.
But as the words kept battering
    away
At my guilty heart
I finally circled them with red
    ink.
Now, Lord, please help me to
    obey them.
Remind me daily, hourly
That listening is a discipline
And a discipline always costs.

I know I must pay a price.
The price for me
Is a listening ear
And a quiet tongue.

My dear brothers and sisters, be quick to listen, slow to speak, and
slow to get angry.   James 1:19, NLT

July 21

A Woman of Compassion

A woman of compassion seeks first, always first, the kingdom of God and his righteousness, knowing that all else will be given to her. She has one single purpose: to know and do the will of God. Often she narrows her interests in order to expand her heart for others.

She says to her troubled friend, "I feel your pain in my heart. I don't have a cure-all kit, but I will walk through the dark tunnel with you until the light breaks through again."

She says to her reserved husband, "I understand that you don't want to talk now, but I'm here for you if I can help."

She listens to the outbursts of her children in a way that makes them feel secure. She reminds them of their priceless individuality.

She opens her home as well as her heart. She knows that a cup of hot tea and an hour of concerned listening means so much more than "We want to have you for dinner someday."

A woman of compassion rests her total self on the reliability of the Word of God. Consequently she does not live in pieces—she lives in peace.

The Lord is good to all; he has compassion on all he has made.

Psalm 145:9, NIV

The You Means Me

O my Father, my Father!
At this crisis time of my life
When I feel trampled and battered
I know it is imperative
For me to remember
That the nature of my problem
Is not the significant thing.
The significant thing
Is the nature of You
My refuge. My rock.
My high tower.
There is no situation
Anytime, or anywhere
Of which I cannot confidently say
"For this I have Him."
But I am so quick to forget
And so prone to neglect.
Lord, may I get it settled
Once and for all
That when You say
"My peace I give unto you"
The *you* means *me!*

I am leaving you with a gift—peace of mind and heart. And the peace
I give isn't like the peace the world gives. So don't be troubled or
afraid.

John 14:27, NLT

July 23

God, Hold Me Close

O God

Hold me close

While I cry

For my freedom.

The louder I shout

The deeper my soul

Needs to know

You will never, never

Let me go.

Lost Argument

I read this morning
Your direct and piercing question
To the ancient Job:
"Do you still want to argue
With the Almighty?
Or will you yield?"
With thoughtful heart
I read Job's wise reply:
"I am nothing. . . .
How could I find the answers?
I lay my hand upon my mouth in silence."
You know so well that I do, God.
I continue to argue with You
As though I were in charge.
As though I could solve my own dilemma.
Finally in the end, broken and defeated
I yield to You, and then—peace.
Forgive me, dear God
For so foolishly ending
Where I should have begun.

Woe to him who quarrels with his Maker, to him who is but a
potsherd among the potsherds on the ground. Does the clay say to
the potter, "What are you making?" Does your work say, "He has
no hands"?
Isaiah 45:9, NIV

July 25

Every Valley Exalted

Sometimes, Lord

It seems as though

You are the God of the hills

But not of the valleys.

For these past months

I have lived in a dark, lonely valley.

But then I remember Your promise

That every valley shall be exalted.

God, help me to persevere, to endure

Until my personal valley

Is gloriously exalted.

Every valley shall be raised up, every mountain and hill made low; the rough ground shall become level, the rugged places a plain. And the glory of the Lord will be revealed, and all mankind together will see it. For the mouth of the Lord has spoken.   Isaiah 40:4-5, NIV

$\mathcal{J}$ u l y 2 6

Immediately

Dear Lord
I'm so tired of living
In my little cramped vessel—
So weary of dangling my feet in the water
But never stepping out of the boat.
I want to walk the waves with You
Just as Peter did.
True, he took only a few steps
Before losing his courage
But at least he was heading toward You.
Lord, I'm coming, too!
If I begin to falter or sink
I trust You to catch me
Just as You caught Peter.
Remember, Lord?
You caught him *immediately*.

But when he looked around at the high waves, he was terrified and
began to sink. "Save me, Lord!" he shouted. Instantly Jesus reached
out his hand and grabbed him. "You don't have much faith," Jesus
said. "Why did you doubt me?"   Matthew 14:30-31, NLT

The Promise

O dear God, I continue to believe
Your personal promise still stands
Though every quivering emotion within
Shouts that it will be broken.
I am claiming Your help through the wilderness
Despite every frightening shadow and vale.
Often you do the most
When You seem to do the least.
Sometimes secretly
Sometimes quietly
Often slowly
But always most certainly
You are true to Your word.
And so, my Lord
Though I am weak, weary, and worn
Help me not to despair.
You see me, You hear me.
You know I am depending utterly
Upon Your unblemished integrity
Surely You will keep Your word.

The Lord is my shepherd, I shall not be in want. He makes me lie
down in green pastures, he leads me beside quiet waters, he restores
my soul. He guides me in paths of righteousness for his name's sake.

Psalm 23:1-3, NIV

July 28

Stephanie

More than anything else she wanted to play the piano. Her mother called to ask if I would give her lessons. "But I must tell you one thing: Stephanie is fighting an advanced malignancy. Her left arm has been amputated. Her future is critical."

I was startled. How could I teach a little girl with one arm to play the piano? Her mother's words kept echoing . . . "More than anything else she wants to take lessons from you."

God, please help me to teach her the music of love.

On her first lesson, she came with her shiny red book. Her eyes sparkled. She could hardly wait! Week after week we sat at the piano learning notes, playing melodies—she with her right hand, I with my left.

"I'm Mrs. Treble," she told me. "You're Mr. Bass." It was a happy joke between us.

"We're really good together," Stephanie said one day, "But you know what? I could never do it alone."

Stephanie taught me an incredible lesson: When I follow God's instructions, we make beautiful music together. *But I could never do it alone!*

Stephanie is with Jesus now. What joy it must be for her to play with both hands!

Jesus said, "Let the children come to me. Don't stop them! For the Kingdom of Heaven belongs to such as these." Matthew 19:14, NLT

July 29

O God ... My God

O God . . . *My* God
Though You now seem totally hidden
I am clinging to You hopefully
Even confidently.
Someday, some way, You will make
All You are now permitting
Blessedly clear.
With fixed purpose, dear God
I am determined to wait, to trust
To rely upon Your faithfulness.
Despite the drain and strain
I anticipate new perspectives
And fresh depths of insight
Into all that is now so mysterious.
O God, in ways unanticipated
You are teaching me the great truth
Of Samuel Rutherford's words:
"I see that grace grows best in winter."
Thank You, dear God
Thank You for that!

And the God of all grace, who called you to his eternal glory in
Christ, after you have suffered a little while, will himself restore
you and make you strong, firm and steadfast.   1 Peter 5:10, NIV

July 30

Sudden Awe

My face wind-lashed

With stinging sand

Alone I trudge the beach

Filled with sudden awe

That You, O God

Are mightier by far

Than all the breakers

Pounding on the seashores

Of the world.

He gave the sea its boundaries and locked the oceans in vast
reservoirs. Let everyone in the world fear the Lord, and let
everyone stand in awe of him. For when he spoke, the world
began! It appeared at his command.   Psalm 33:7-9, NLT

July 31

The End of the Rope

O dear God

I feel as though I am clinging

To a rough, swinging rope.

Beneath me there is only emptiness.

My hands are bruised and bleeding.

There is no possible way

For me to tie a knot

At the end of the rope

And hang on.

O God, please help me.

Frightened child

Just let go.

I'll catch you.

Do not abandon me, Lord. Do not stand at a distance, my God.
Come quickly to help me, O Lord my savior. Psalm 38:21-22, NLT

August

The Promise of His Presence

God is:

- *Utterly trustworthy*

- *Supremely loving*

- *Always available*

Your Father already knows your needs. He will give you all you need from day to day if you make the Kingdom of God your primary concern.   Luke 12:30-31, NLT

August 1

Why?

Standing here

At the kitchen sink

My hands immersed

In soapsuds

All of a sudden I know

With fresh, penetrating force

I am only really whole

When I am wholly Yours.

Yet with proud self-assertion

I often choose to be

Incomplete.

Why, Lord?

Yes, I am the vine; you are the branches. Those who remain in me,
and I in them, will produce much fruit. For apart from me you can do
nothing.
John 15:5, NLT

August 2

Morning Star

You who are

The Bright and Morning Star

Come in radiant splendor

And flood each shadowed crevice

Of my sullen heart

Until the world shall know

I've touched a Star.

God is light; in him there is no darkness at all. 1 John 1:5, NIV

Tic-Tac-Toe

Sometimes, Lord

I get the impression

We're playing a game

Of tic-tac-toe.

I draw my X

You draw Your O.

Then just as I contemplate

The next move

You draw a straight line

Which finishes the game.

You always win, Lord

Always.

Is it because Your circle

Is Whole

Complete

Total

Like You?

We may throw the dice, but the Lord determines how they fall.

Proverbs 16:33, NLT

Who, Me?

Lord
All of a sudden today
You picked me up
And hugged me
And hugged me
For no discernible reason.
I was puzzled.
After all—
I hadn't picked up my toys
Or practiced my lessons
Or brought You a daisy bouquet—

Hesitantly, I asked why.
You smiled and said:
I love you, that's all.
Then You added:
I long to hug you more often.
Why don't You, Lord?
You are too busy.
Too busy, Lord?
Too busy hugging yourself.

We love because he first loved us.   1 John 4:19, NIV

August 5

Lord

It's wonderful

That You see me

More wonderful

That You lead me

Most wonderful

That You love me.

Good, better, best?

No—with You

All is superlative:

Always best.

Whatever is good and perfect comes to us from God above, who
created all heaven's lights. Unlike them, he never changes or casts
shifting shadows.   James 1:17, NLT

August 6

Best Friends

Lord

Today I read

"And Abraham believed God . . .

And he was called

The friend of God."

Please, Lord, give me

A faith so strong

That we may be

Very best friends!

And so a whole nation came from this one man, Abraham, who was too old to have any children—a nation with so many people that, like the stars of the sky and the sand on the seashore, there is no way to count them.

Hebrews 11:12, NLT

August 7

Can You Sing in the Rain?

When I was a child I loved to take long walks with my tall, loving father. We trudged through meadows, we climbed rolling hills, and often we walked through tree-lined parks. As we walked, Dad would tell me stories about his childhood, and I would ask countless questions about my grandparents.

One day on a country road we walked under a gentle mist of rain. In the distance we saw a sparrow perched on a tree branch. The tiny bird was just singing away. My father asked a question: "Could you sing in the rain if nobody saw and nobody heard but God?"

Years have passed since that long-ago day. There have been wonderful days of joy. And there have been days of tears, too. Sometimes in the darkest night, during the most severe storm, God has enabled me to sing in the rain when nobody saw and nobody heard but God. Even through tears God has reminded me that the longest storm the world has ever known came to an end one sunny morning. And after the storm—a rainbow! God did it for Noah . . . and he does it for us!

Sing to him, sing praise to him; tell of all his wonderful acts.

Psalm 105:2, NIV

August 8

He Said—She Said

Another marriage is shattered, Lord.
The divorce will be final next week.

He said it was the breakdown of communication
And the subtle infiltration of boredom.
She said it was an accumulation of things.
He said she was unnecessarily preoccupied
With home and children and activities.
She said he stifled her dreams
And ignored her achievements.
He said he felt imprisoned, restricted—
That night after night he got the old push-away.
She said he was harsh and brutal
And he often embarrassed her in public.
He said her critical attitudes
Contributed to his sense of inadequacy.
She said she felt lonely and unappreciated
With no claim to personal identity.
He said she wallowed in self-pity
And refused to acknowledge her benefits.
She said he was thriftless and irresponsible.
He said she didn't understand.
She said he didn't care.

Lord, how tragic.
Through all the wearisome years
Neither of them asked what *You* said.

He did evil because he had not set his heart on seeking the Lord.
2 Chronicles 12:14, NIV

Direct Answer

O Lord

I've battled and struggled

I've dragged through

Tortured guilt-ridden hours

I've wept before You

Until there are no more tears.

What more can I do?

Dear child

You can begin to obey!

I assure you, anyone who obeys my teaching will never die!

John 8:51, NLT

August 10

"Have a Nice Forever"

Even at longest, Lord
Life is fleetingly short—
A mere breath
A withering flower
A shadow in pantomime.
It sobers me
That I am but a passing occupant
A temporary guest who says hello
Then so suddenly—good-bye.

But, Lord
You have chosen me
To be Your very own.
The instant You call my name
I shall be a permanent resident
In my Father's house.
Once again
With ecstatic joy
I shall say hello—
But never through all Eternity
Shall I have to say good-bye!

There are many rooms in my Father's home, and I am going to
prepare a place for you. If this were not so, I would tell you plainly.
When everything is ready, I will come and get you, so that you will
always be with me where I am.

John 14:2-3, NLT

August 11

Precious Treasure

O dear Lord

How can You know all about me—

Everything I've ever done—

And still love me so extravagantly?

You treat me as if I were

A precious treasure or something.

The beautiful part is—

To You I am!

For the Lord takes delight in his people; he crowns the humble with salvation.
Psalm 149:4, NIV

August 12

Beautiful Fact

Lord

There are countless things in my life

That are inexcusable.

There are things unaccountable

And things unexplainable.

There are things irrefutable

And things irresponsible.

But it comes to me with unutterable relief

That because of Your amazing love

Nothing in my life is unforgivable.

Our old sinful selves were crucified with Christ so that sin might lose
its power in our lives. We are no longer slaves to sin.   Romans 6:6, NLT

August 13

Spiritual Tug-of-War

Lord, I've waited long enough

No longer can I withstand

This spiritual tug-of-war between us.

Today I will do what You asked me to do.

I still don't want to, Lord—

Surely You know that.

I'm frightened and ill-at-ease.

I feel foolish and uncomfortable.

I almost feel put-upon.

What You've asked of me slaps at my pride.

Nevertheless, I choose to obey You

Simply because I love You.

Do You understand, dear Lord?

I wouldn't do this

For anyone in the world—but You.

You are good, and what you do is good; teach me your decrees.

Psalm 119:68, NIV

On the Way to the Airport

The women's retreat had ended, and I was on my way out the door. I had only a little while to get to the airport for my plane trip home. As I hurried toward the waiting car, a charming young wife followed me. I sensed her deep anxiety when she asked, "How can I live before my husband who wants nothing to do with God?"

From the car window I said, "Let me give you four DON'TS and four DO'S:

1. DON'T push.
2. DON'T preach.
3. DON'T pretend.
4. DON'T puncture his self-esteem.

1. DO permeate your home with love.
2. DO practice forgiving.
3. DO pay compliments to him often.
4. DO persist in prayer.

"Oh, yes, one more DON'T: Don't ever, ever, ever give up!"

The young woman reached inside her purse for her personal card. With gentle persuasion she asked, "Would you be willing to write all of that down for me when you get home?" I promised I would.

We've never seen each other again, but almost a year after the retreat I found her short note in our mailbox. Just three words and her name. "Thanks! It's working!"

Find out what is pleasing to the Lord. Ephesians 5:10, NLT

August 15

New Bible

This was an exciting day for me, Lord!
This morning I opened my new Bible.
Not a single word was circled
Not a single phrase underlined.
Now with each new day
I can circle and underline again
I can word-clutter the margins
And I know what will happen, Lord—
I'll be asking as I read
Why didn't I see that before?
But even with the joy of a new Bible
I'm going to miss my old one
With its tattered pages—
It's creased and torn edges.
Oh, how many personal notes
Are jotted on the margins
How many God-whispered secrets.
Yes, Lord, I'll miss it.
But thank You for a friend's reminder:
"If your Bible is falling apart
Chances are your life isn't."

Your word is a lamp for my feet and a light for my path.
Psalm 119:105, NLT

Need of Patience

O God
How pointedly You speak to my
   heart
When You say, "You have need
   of patience . . ."
Remorsefully I acknowledge Your
   truth
For there is nothing I need more.
I am so easily disturbed, Lord
So many little things annoy me.
Patience is simply not a virtue
   of mine.

I'm impatient with our neighbor
Who mows his lawn but once every
   six weeks.
I'm impatient with our newsboy
Every time he misses our front
   porch.
Yesterday a friend kept me waiting
And I robed my impatience in
   self-pity.

Shoes pushed under the bed
An unrinsed coffee cup
An overly detailed story
Toys scattered on our lawn—
How I murmur and fret.
(Sometimes I explode.)

I'm impatient with myself, Lord
My foolish mistakes, my failures
And often I'm impatient with
   You.
I am like a petulant child
Who insists on an answer—*now*.

Yes, God, I have need of patience.
But I will not be discouraged
Nor will I continue to flog myself.
Again Your Word speaks
   pointedly:
"My God shall supply all your
   need . . ."
The very need You know I have
Is the very need You will supply.
You will renew me in patience.
In You there is hope!

Since God chose you to be the holy people whom he loves, you must clothe yourselves with tenderhearted mercy, kindness, humility, gentleness, and patience. You must make allowance for each other's faults and forgive the person who offends you. Remember, the Lord forgave you, so you must forgive others.   Colossians 3:12-13, NLT

August 17

You Name the Stars

God, I walked alone

In Your beautiful time

Called Night.

I lifted my face

To the soft-pillowed sky

And watched a shivering star

Fall out of bed—

And then I remembered:

That very star

You call by name!

He determines the number of the stars and calls them each by name. Great is our Lord and mighty in power; his understanding has no limit.

Psalm 147:4-5, NIV

August 18

The Difference

O dear God

Help me to grow

More like You

In spite of my circumstances.

Wounded child

You will grow

More like Me

Because of your circumstances.

Consider it pure joy, my brothers, whenever you face trials of many kinds, because you know that the testing of your faith develops perseverance.

James 1:2-3, NIV

August 19

Praise upon Praise

O Father

Through the years

You have permitted

Hurt upon hurt

In my God-planned life.

This early morning

Even before I greet the dawn

I offer You

Praise upon praise

For You are transforming every hurt

Into a holy hallmark—

A genuine guarantee

Of my permanent identification

With You.

Before I was afflicted I went astray, but now I obey your word.

Psalm 119:67, NIV

August 20

I Stake My Life

I stake my life totally

Completely

Permanently

On the integrity of Jesus.

Lord, Your integrity means

You will do all You promised.

You will see me through

Every fiery furnace

Every tempestuous storm.

If not, dear God

Then nothing in life

Makes any sense whatever.

Your part is to perform

What You promised.

My part is to trust and obey.

Obey me, and I will be your God and you will be my people.
Walk in all the ways I command you, that it may go well with you.
Jeremiah 7:23, NIV

He Is Enough

She lived in the most deprived section of the crowded city of New York, where there was never enough of anything—never enough food or clothing, never enough warmth or shelter, never enough compassion.

But one day a benevolent young couple invited her to spend a week at the seashore, to experience a piece of life she had never known. Hour by hour she breathed deeply as the crashing waves brushed against her small frame. She looked at the vast expanse of water—and then, without warning she began to sob. For the first time in her life she saw something of which there was enough!

Today I ask forgiveness for my limited concept of God. At times I've secretly felt cheated—as though somehow He was not enough to satisfy the longings of my heart. I need to learn and relearn that in Him there is enough faithfulness, enough love, enough grace, enough joy! May I never forget that God Himself is now and forever my great *enough!*

You will show me the way of life, granting me the joy of your presence and the pleasures of living with you forever.   Psalm 16:11, NLT

Sane Estimate

Lord, help me to face with honesty
And genuine appreciation
The talents and abilities
You have given
As special gifts to me.
Give me a sane estimate of myself.
Neither exaggerated nor mud-crawling.
Just *sane*, as Your Word admonishes.
May I be joyfully satisfied
With Your unique plan for me.
When at times I'd secretly love to ride
On a colorful float
Beautifully adorned
Waving to cheering crowds
Smile at me, Lord.
With a twinkle in Your eye
Remind me again
That somebody has to build the float.

For by the grace given me I say to every one of you: Do not think
of yourself more highly than you ought, but rather think of yourself
with sober judgment, in accordance with the measure of faith God
has given you.   Romans 12:3, NIV

August 23

Morbid Memories

Lord, I can't mow down morbid memories

Like my husband mows tall grass.

Mercilessly they take revenge

By tramping gleefully

Through my somber heart.

So, dear Lord

I ask YOU to shake them

In the sunlight of Your love.

Then may the gentle breeze

Of the Holy Spirit

Blow them all away—

Never to be found again.

Fix your thoughts on what is true and honorable and right. Think about things that are pure and lovely and admirable. Think about things that are excellent and worthy of praise. Philippians 4:8, NLT

Beautiful Things Happen

O God
Such beautiful things happen
When I meet You day by day
In quietness and confidence.
There is a deep inner wholeness
And the assurance of Your guidance.
I am not so easily disturbed
By changing circumstances.
I am less dependent on others
And more dependent on You.
My eyes may be full of tears
But my heart is full of joy.
In discovering Your hidden treasures
I learn how deeply I am treasured by You.
When day by day I am responsive
To Your whispered secrets
You do more for me in one day
Than I could do for myself in a lifetime.

You have given me greater joy than those who have abundant harvests
of grain and wine. I will lie down in peace and sleep, for you alone,
O Lord, will keep me safe.   Psalm 4:7-8, NLT

August 25

Foolish Child

O God

Why do You play

A threatening game

Of hide-and-seek with me

When I know You are there?

Foolish child

It is not hide-and-seek.

It is only SEEK.

Seek Me with all your heart.

You will surely find Me.

Never do I play games

With My cherished children.

If you, then, though you are evil, know how to give good gifts to your children, how much more will your Father in heaven give good gifts to those who ask him!

Matthew 7:11, NIV

August 26

Relentless

God, You are relentless.

I have yielded

Everything to You—

Everything but one small exception—

An exception so small

I'm truly amazed

You would even take notice.

Yet it is invariably

To that one small exception

That You keep bringing me

Back, and back, and back.

Why does it matter so much to You?

My child

Why does it matter so much to you?

Then he said to the crowd, "If any of you wants to be my follower,
you must put aside your selfish ambition, shoulder your cross daily,
and follow me. If you try to keep your life for yourself, you will lose
it. But if you give up your life for me, you will find true life."

Luke 9:23-24, NLT

So Slowly

Lord

I seem to grow so slowly

So *very* slowly.

So thank You for reminding me

That never has a Master Musician

Composed a lasting symphony

In an hour.

For God knew his people in advance, and he chose them to become like his Son, so that his Son would be the firstborn, with many brothers and sisters.

Romans 8:29, NLT

Knowing God Intimately

How do we learn to know God so intimately that all of life takes on a new freshness?

We acknowledge that God is the instigator. We would not be wanting him if he did not first want us. Even a glimmer of spiritual desire is *his* desire planted in us.

We resign from our self-appointed office as president of the "Me First Club," which gives God the privilege of saying, "Good! Now I'll promote you."

We focus on Jesus Christ, God's Son. It is never a matter of how conspicuous we are. It only matters that he is conspicuous in us.

We make no promise of perfection. All the perfection we'll ever have is the perfection of Jesus living in us.

We let God's Word saturate our hearts. Five or ten minutes each day is far more helpful than three hours once a week.

We trust God to do within us what we cannot do, knowing that he is able to do immeasurably more than all we ask or imagine, according to his power that is at work within us.

To him who is able to do immeasurably more than all we ask or imagine, according to his power that is at work within us, to him be glory in the church and in Christ Jesus throughout all generations, for ever and ever! Amen.   Ephesians 3:20-21, NIV

August 29

I'm Here

God, I cannot see You
But I wait for You.

My child
I can see you
And I'm here.

In the morning, O Lord, you hear my voice; in the morning I lay my
requests before you and wait in expectation.   Psalm 5:3, NIV

The Answer

Lord, my life seems
So full of things
I can't do anything about.

True, dear child
But I will do something
With *those things.*

Therefore, I urge you, brothers, in view of God's mercy, to offer you
bodies as living sacrifices, holy and pleasing to God—this is your
spiritual act of worship.   Romans 12:1, NIV

August 31

The Conclusion

Lord, Lord
I am not as brave
As You seem to think
Nor as strong
Nor as capable of standing firm
In the midst of affliction.
Lord, there is not a drop
Of emotional response in me.
No awareness of Your love
No comfort or joy in Your promises.
I have no deep conviction
That You are real.
There is no daylight in my heart
Nor even candlelight.
Nevertheless, with sheer determination
And perhaps a bit of spiritual grit
I have opted to throw my weight
On Your word *without*
Rather than my feelings *within*.
I don't know exactly when it happened
But I have reached the conclusion
That I would rather walk with You
In the dark of night
Than walk without You
In the light.

Come, people of Israel, let us walk in the light of the Lord!

Isaiah 2:5, NLT

September

The Promise of Stability

He will hold me in his steady hand.

No turn in the affairs of my life

can baffle him.

The Lord Almighty is here among us; the God of Israel
is our fortress.   Psalm 46:11, NLT

September 1

John 15:5

Lord
Often You come in the nick of time
Before I collide with a crisis—

Yesterday
There I was
Rushing
Dashing madly
Company coming for dinner
The table unset
The salad half made
My hair in wild hysteria
And You interrupted
With Your quiet plea:
"Let Me help you."

It was better after that, Lord—
From boil to simmer
Far less hectic
My head stayed on.
Just one more incident
To prove I can't do anything
Without You.

You said so first.

In him we live and move and exist.   Acts 17:28, NLT

September 2

Indelible Ink

I love her exuberance, Lord
Her refreshing spontaneity.
I smile when I think
How she rushed into the house
(Blue eyes aglow)
And thrust her new book
Into my hands:
"Please write my name on my book
In great big letters
So everybody knows
It belongs to me."

Yes, Lord
Yes.
I want that too.
Write Your name
On the chapters of my life—
My thoughts
Motives
Secret dreams . . .
Write Your name
On my total being
So everybody knows
I belong to You.

And Lord
Indelible ink, please.

You are not your own; you were bought at a price.
I Corinthians 6:19-20, NIV

September 3

Method of Achievement

I said to You:

Lord, crush my resentment

Chisel my rebellion

Chain my self-centeredness

Crash my inconsistency

Stifle my fears.

You said to me:

I will cleanse you with My blood

I will melt you with My Love

I will flood you with Myself

Until you grasp anew—

Our intention is the same

But the method is Mine.

Who is able to advise the Spirit of the Lord? Who knows enough to be his teacher or counselor? Has the Lord ever needed anyone's advice? Does he need instruction about what is good or what is best?

Isaiah 40:13-14, NLT

September 4

Master Artist

There are days, Lord
Frightening and mysterious
When You seem to splash across
The canvas of my heart
With wasted strokes—
Like an amateur artist
Carelessly mixing pigment.
Frankly
Your colors appear unblended
Your strokes haphazard.
Instead of design
I see blobs of distortion.
Today, Lord
This very hour
Dissolve my apprehension
Renew my confidence
Settle my conviction
That You have planned
The total design.
Finally, Lord
When the finished canvas
Is luminously displayed
Make this my song of affirmation:
The pattern is perfectly clear.

"For I know the plans I have for you," says the Lord. "They are
plans for good and not for disaster, to give you a future and a hope."
Jeremiah 29:11, NLT

September 5

Hold Me to My Yes

I'm frightened, Lord
Bewildered
What shall I do?
I could have sworn I was free—
Free from the sinister
    temptation
So fiercely threatening me.

Months have passed
Even years
Not once have old memories
    haunted me
Nor has ugliness plagued me
Until now.
Suddenly
Tauntingly
Daringly
Desire steals in
Like a midnight thief.

It clutches
Crushes
Until my thoughts reel
Until my breath is tight.

Lord, the day I said *yes* to You
My total being responded.
This You know.
Now while the enemy seeks
The target of my heart
Don't let me renege—
Hold me to my yes.

For this we both know:
To sacrifice the ultimate
For the immediate
Spells disaster
Despair
Defeat.

So, if you think you are standing firm, be careful that you don't fall!
No temptation has seized you except what is common to man. And
God is faithful; he will not let you be tempted beyond what you can
bear. But when you are tempted, he will also provide a way out so
that you can stand up under it.   1 Corinthians 10:12-13, NIV

September 6

Sacrilege

"That was great, my friend."

(Why wasn't I asked to do it?)

"Congratulations on your achievement."

(Why does he always succeed?)

"Your new home is charming."

(Some people have everything.)

Forgive me, God

For moments of sacrilege

When I have expressed good

While thinking evil.

A heart at peace gives life to the body, but envy rots the bones.

Proverbs 14:30, NIV

September 7

Competition with God

Often we must ask, what is my competition with God? When life seems to stand still, when my thoughts saunter through blind alleys, those very *thoughts* become my competition with God. When I embrace my personal desires instead of giving allegiance to God, *desire* becomes my competition with God. When I waste valuable time, ignoring God-assigned tasks, *time* becomes my competition with God. When personal possessions erase my concern for a desperately needy world, *possessions* become my competition with God.

If we allow a controversy in our lives, our praying may be with pretense, but it will not be with power. Walking the path of self-indulgence eventually leads to emptiness. Seeking *first* the Kingdom of God and his righteousness leads to freedom and joy.

You will hear a voice say, "This is the way; turn around and walk here."

Isaiah 30:21, NLT

September 8

Why?

I'm singing today
In the midst of adversity—
Singing without reason for song.
Lord, do You want to know why?
Simply because I'm staunchly convinced
That as I continue my songs in the night
You'll create a new reason for singing.

He put a new song in my mouth, a hymn of praise to our God. Many
will see and fear and put their trust in the Lord.   Psalm 40:3, NIV

September 9

Moments of Leisure

Lord, thank You
For the moments of leisure
And peaceful solitude
I can legitimately snatch
Here and there
Without apologizing.
Thank You for assuring me
That I needn't condemn myself
When I spend some time
Reading or resting
Or shopping just for fun.
Thank You for convincing me
That there's no glory
In a rat race.
I've discovered, dear Lord
That an hour or two
"Away from it all"
Calms my inner muddle
And cuts through the confusion.

Without a driving sense of urgency
I think more clearly—
I plan more wisely.
I am more patient, more loving
More understanding with my
    family.
I even accept with calmness
The multiple demands imposed
    upon me.

Thank You so much, dear God
For the certain knowledge that
    Jesus
(Who always obeyed the Father)
Went apart from the crowd to rest.
So must I!

He said to them, "Come with me by yourselves to a quiet place and get some rest."
                                                    Mark 6:31, NIV

I Keep Running Back to You

You know how it is with me, Lord:
So often I mess up my days.
I judge harshly
I am critical and obstinate
I waste time and energy
I blame others for my failure.
There are people I try to avoid
And tasks I try to evade
And when I can't have my own way
I sulk in my own little corner.
Lord, I even turn my back on You
To escape Your penetrating gaze.

Then finally I get fed up with
    myself.
The intolerable loneliness
    frightens me
And I can no longer endure my
    shame.
It always happens, Lord—
I keep running back to You!

Where else can I go?
Who else understands me so well
Or forgives me so totally?
Who else can save me from foolish
    pride?
No one, Lord, but You.
So thank You for accepting me
For loving me
For always welcoming me.
I just can't help it, Lord
I keep running back to You!

He tends his flock like a shepherd: He gathers the lambs in his arms and carries them close to his heart; he gently leads those that have young.

Isaiah 40:11, NIV

One of the Two

Dear God

Please help me.

I'm encumbered with problems

Too heavy to handle.

Dear child

Why should two of us

Carry the weight of your burden

When one of the two is Me?

Cast all your anxiety on him because he cares for you.   1 Peter 5:7, NIV

September 12

Seek First

O Lord
How futile, how foolish
To attempt to keep up with the Joneses
On the gold-studded ladder of success.
Even if we make it
(Setting high, competitive goals)
We awake one dismal morning
To discover the Smiths have bypassed the Joneses
So it starts again—the goading competition.

God, Your objective is far more rewarding.
You want us to "keep up" with Your Plan
For our individual lives.
"Seek first the Kingdom of God"
Is Your shining word to us.
Forgive us for moments and days
(Even months)
When our love of money
Has exceeded our love for You.
Please, God
Be our Financial Advisor
And deliver us from a thousand "if onlys."
May we never be defeated
By the lack of money
Or captivated by the lure of it.

So if we have enough food and clothing, let us be content. But
people who long to be rich fall into temptation and are trapped by
many foolish and harmful desires that plunge them into ruin and
destruction.   1 Timothy 6:8-9, NLT

September 13

Lord, Remind Me Often Today

Lord, remind me often today . . .

That if there is some area in my life
Not fully surrendered to You
That is always the area
In which I will be most severely tried.

Lord, remind me often today . . .

That You've already done Your part:
You've provided a way of escape
Against every temptation I shall face.
I must *choose* Your escape-door.

Lord, remind me often today . . .

That You want more than first place
In my heart and life.
You want all of me, always.
Surrender means every detail of my life
Under your careful scrutiny.

Lord, remind me often today . . .

That You alone are my Source.
Only God
Always God
Totally God
You alone are my Source.

He must become greater; I must become less.   John 3:30, NIV

September 14

The God Who Never Changes

It is irrefutably true: We have lost many opportunities that can never be retrieved. We have made foolish choices that can never be rectified. But we dare not live life in a spirit of despair and defeat.

As children of God we need to understand that all God's discipline has but one objective: To bring us to the end of ourselves and back to him! His desire is always to restore us, never to reject us. His goal is always to use us, never to ignore us.

With confession, renewed surrender, and a heart that is fixed on him, God will do in us whatever he needs to do to make us whatever he wants us to be. Every necessary change God chooses to make is wonderfully possible because of Jesus, who never changes.

Jesus Christ is the same yesterday, today, and forever.

Hebrews 13:8, NLT

The Challenge

It may be true, dear God
That my husband and I had more to live on
A year ago than we have today
But it is equally true
That we have just as much to live *for*.
The real values of our lives remain
Solid, stable, unshifting.
Our financial loss has in no way
Diminished the value of a single friendship.
We have lost nothing of human dignity
And we are discovering spiritual realities
Full of wonder and sheer delight.
Our faith in Your loving-kindness
Adds growing serenity to our guided lives.
You are making us increasingly aware
That what we *are* is vastly more vital
Than our fondest possessions.
Above all, You are teaching us
That a limited salary is our shining challenge
To trust and exalt our limitless God!

So don't worry about having enough food or drink or clothing. Why be like the pagans who are so deeply concerned about these things? Your heavenly Father already knows all your needs, and he will give you all you need from day to day if you live for him and make the Kingdom of God your primary concern.   Matthew 6:31-33, NLT

Permanent Hookup

God

I am always getting one thing

Straightened out with You

And then another lion

Jumps out of the jungle.

Why couldn't You create

Some kind of permanent hookup

So life would stay

Settled, serene

And ecstatically spiritual?

Dear child

I have.

It's called Heaven.

And they will see his face, and his name will be written on their foreheads. And there will be no night there—no need for lamps or sun—for the Lord God will shine on them. And they will reign forever and ever.

Revelation 22:4-5, NLT

September 17

That Little

O dear God

There is within me

A deep, intense longing

To use whatever gifts

You've entrusted to me.

But, Lord, they seem so small.

There's so little I can do

So little I can say.

My timid child

It is just "that little"

That I ask from you.

Hear what I say:

OBEY!

It is the Lord your God you must follow, and him you must revere.
Keep his commands and obey him; serve him and hold fast to him.

Deuteronomy 13:4, NIV

September 18

Fear Not

Again and again, dear Lord
I read Your words, "Fear not."
Surely You would not say it so often
If there were any reason to fear.
Nor would You command it so explicitly
If You could not keep me from fearing.
God, You have given me a *Fear Not*
For every puzzling circumstance
For every possible emergency
For every trial and testing
Real or imagined.
Yet I confess wasted hours—
Even days, dear Lord
When fear clutches and clobbers me
Until I am physically and emotionally spent.
Lord, when David cried to You
You delivered him from all his fears.
On this gray-sky morning
I kneel before You with David's cry.
O my Father, I cannot believe
You would be less kind to me
Than You were to David.

Those who look to him for help will be radiant with joy; no shadow of
shame will darken their faces. I cried out to the Lord in my suffering,
and he heard me. He set me free from all my fears.   Psalm 34:5-6, NLT

September 19

Greater Understanding

O God
With greater understanding
My heart proclaims
Your own words:
"For my thoughts are not your thoughts
Neither are your ways my ways . . ."

What so often seems to me
An enormous trial
Crushing, mangling
Tearing me to shreds
Represents to You
An enormous transformation
Of my total self—
Purging, renewing
Liberating me
Until my soul soars!

"For my thought are not your thoughts, neither are your ways my ways," declares the Lord. "As the heavens are higher than the earth, so are my ways higher than your ways and my thoughts than your thoughts."

Isaiah 55:8-9, NIV

Commonplace Days

Lord of my commonplace days
Forgive me for foolishly waiting
For "divine inspiration"
Before moving in on the tasks
Personally assigned to me.
Hopefully I am learning
To face with greater determination
The day-by-day drudgery
The trite, mundane tasks
The pushing-pulling glamourless duties.
Lord, even when I think
I'm getting no place
Keep me pushing on and on
With purpose and direction.
Grab my heart and quiet me
When I begin to whine and whimper.
Despite the daily drain
I think I see it more clearly now:
It is only when I begin to *do*
That You begin to *bless.*

And whatever you do, whether in word or deed, do it all in the name
of the Lord Jesus, giving thanks to God the Father through him.

Colossians 3:17, NIV

A Listening Heart

I remember vividly the lesson I learned from my husband one day as he came home from his office weary and depleted. It had been a difficult day. He needed to talk.

My day had been difficult, too. Countless interruptions, phone calls, guests coming for brunch the next day. I wanted to listen, so I suggested that he follow me from room to room while I dusted furniture.

We tried it. While I dusted the piano, he talked. When I cleaned the clanging piano keys he continued, but with a trace of impatience. Next the stereo, then the tables. When I moved, he moved. Suddenly he grabbed my shoulders. "Please listen to me!"

Frankly I was shocked. "Honey, I heard every word you said."

"I mean listen with your *heart!*" I dropped the dust cloth. We sat down, and I gave my full attention. No body signals, no folded arms, no finger tapping. I was again aware of the tremendous responsibilities my husband carried. He needed my understanding. He thanked me profusely for listening.

That night I remembered how often God had said to the children of Israel, "If my people would only listen." I thought of God's yearning for an intimate relationship with us. He waits for our response to his still small voice. He longs for our listening hearts. How we must grieve him when we don't listen!

Be still, and know that I am God.   Psalm 46:10, NIV

I Sing in the Rain

One cold, misty day
When I was nine years old
I walked hand-in-hand
Through a wooded forest
With my strong, gentle father.
"Listen to the stillness," he whispered.
"Stillness makes beautiful music."
Suddenly he pointed to a tiny bird
Perched on a limb of a bending tree.
"The bird doesn't know we're here
But he's singing his heart out."
Then smiling down at me he asked
"Could you sing in the rain
If nobody heard you but God?"

Lord, though many years have passed
Since I walked with my father
I have never forgotten his question.
Today I am alone—
Yet not alone, for YOU are here.
Though my heart is grief-drenched
I know You are worthy of praise.
Help me, please help me
To sing my feeble song in the rain
Though nobody hears but You.

Answer me when I call to you, O my righteous God. Give me relief
from my distress; be merciful to me and hear my prayer.   Psalm 4:1, NIV

September 23

Now

My great, strong God!

All the fight

Is drained out of me.

In my debilitating weakness

I can't even hold on to You.

But Your own words

Keep my hope stirring:

"For I your God

Am firmly grasping

Your right hand.

I am saying unto you

Do not fear.

I have become your helper."

Now, dear Lord!

Now!

The Lord is a shelter for the oppressed, a refuge in times of trouble. Those who know your name trust in you, for you, O Lord, have never abandoned anyone who searches for you.   Psalm 9:9-10, NLT

September 24

Relationship

Lord

As You show me

That You are my Father

By instructing me

May I show You

That I am Your child

By obeying You.

This is love for God: to obey his commands.   1 John 5:3, NIV

September 25

Excuses

O God
I've become a self-educated master
Of a thousand polished excuses.
Hoping to avoid Your penetrating gaze
I clutch them to me like valuable gems.
When I think I have myself thoroughly covered
I'm caught short with the realization
That You see right through me.
My flimsy excuses are never really hidden.
I find an excuse for all my failures
Wrong choices
Late appointments
Wasted time.
I excuse my foolish blunders, my laziness
My broken resolves, my unreached goals.
I need Your help, Lord!
To hide from You is as foolish
As the Grand Canyon
Attempting to hide from the sky.
O God, my only hope
Lies in Your invincible power
To make me what I am not yet
But what You know I can become.
Strengthen my will, Lord.
Make me firm, steadfast, consistent.
Control my impulses, my emotions.
May I keep pursuing and never quit.

Let us fix our eyes on Jesus, the author and perfecter of our faith,
who for the joy set before him endured the cross, scorning its shame,
and sat down at the right hand of the throne of God. Hebrews 12:2, NIV

Three Unalterable Truths

Lord, through the years
Of walking hand-in-hand with You
I have learned three unalterable truths:
First, what You command me to do
You consistently expect me to do.
Never do You say, "Give the command a fair try."
Nor do You say, "Consider and then decide."
My natural weakness is never
An acceptable excuse.
Nor is my inability
To reach unreachable standards.
Rather, You tell me to *seek*
And then to *keep* Your commands.
Second, all of Your commands
Are always for my ultimate good.
"Obey Me," Your Word says
"So that I can do for you
All the wonderful things I promised. . . ."
"In the keeping of My Word
There is great reward."
Third, whatever You command me to do
You fully enable me to do.
As You give light to reveal a command
So You give grace to fulfill it.
Your divine energy is always at my disposal.
The choice to obey is always mine.
The power to obey is always Yours.

May I be blameless in keeping your principles; then I will never have
to be ashamed.   Psalm 119:80, NLT

Free Choice

My Lord

Because You have given me

The irrevocable power of free choice

You will not force me

To do something

I selfishly don't want to do.

But I have made

A grave and painful discovery:

You can certainly

Make me wish I had done it.

All of us have strayed away like sheep. We have left God's paths to follow our own. Yet the Lord laid on him the guilt and sins of us all.

Isaiah 53:6, NLT

An Honest Appraisal

I must answer honestly. . . .
Am I often so exhausted that I want to be left alone?
Are my outside activities crowding my availability at home?
Am I tense, irritable, tied in knots?
Am I sometimes preoccupied?
Do I answer questions sharply?
Do I vacillate in my decisions?
Am I unable to cope with simple tasks without showing panic?

If I must answer yes to any or all of the above, I am too busy.
I am burdening my family. I am puzzling my friends. I am
endangering my mental and physical stamina. I am ignoring
God's agenda.

The solution . . .
I must accept the fact that the little word *no* is often more
honoring to God and to those I care about than an impulsive *yes*.

The threatening question . . .
Will I begin to make changes *today*?

I can do everything with the help of Christ who gives me the strength
I need. Philippians 4:13, NLT

At Long Last

O Lord

At long last

I have placed in Your hands

The strong and aching desire

Which for so many months

Completely absorbed me.

Now to my surprise and delight

I have made the joyful discovery

That all my tenacious resistance

Was far more painful, more agonizing

Than a total letting go

In obedience to Your command.

My child

So it will always be.

Seek the Lord, all you humble of the land, you who do what he commands. Seek righteousness, seek humility.   Zephaniah 2:3, NIV

September 30

So Demanding

God, Your Word is so demanding.
It demands great stretches of my
    time—
Not just occasionally
But day after day, year after year.
I can't just grab a bite of it
With one hand in the dishwater
Or on the steering wheel
While I'm backing out of the
    garage.
Your Word insists that I ponder
That I contemplate and meditate
That I seriously apply it to my life.
It insists on obedience and
    forgiveness
On gentleness and love.
Its claim upon me is absolute.
Only as I obey
Can I know the peace
That passes all understanding.

But God
Its very insistence transforms me
For it proclaims Your faithfulness
In superlative terms.
As I give it my fixed, steady
    attention
My composure increases
My anxiety decreases
And I am supported on every side.
Jeremiah said, " . . . your word was
    unto me
The joy and rejoicing of my
    heart."

And in the margin of my Bible
Next to the words of the prophet
There is my own personal
    notation:
"My heart, too!"

Heaven and earth will disappear, but my words will remain forever.
Matthew 24:35, NLT

October

The Promise of Endurance

Lord, help me to avoid stumbling from worry to worry

by teaching me to soar from prayer to prayer.

Those who wait on the Lord will find new strength.
They will fly high on wings like eagles. They will run
and not grow weary. They will walk and not faint.

Isaiah 40:31, NLT

October 1

In the Morning

"Joy comes with the morning" (Psalm 30:5).

Today, Lord
I have an unshakable conviction
A positive resolute assurance
That what You have spoken
Is unalterably true.

But today, Lord
My sick body feels stronger
And the stomping pain quietly subsides.
Tomorrow . . .

And then tomorrow
If I must struggle again
With aching exhaustion
With twisting pain
Until I am breathless
Until I am utterly spent
Until fear eclipses the last vestige of hope
Then, Lord
Then grant me the enabling grace
To believe without feeling
To know without seeing
To clasp Your invisible hand
And wait with invincible trust

For the morning.

Weeping may go on all night, but joy comes with the morning.

Psalm 30:5, NLT

October 2

Ten to One

Lord, I ask more questions
Than You ask.
The ratio, I would suppose
Is ten to one.

I ask:
Why do You permit this anguish?
How long can I endure it?
What possible purpose does it serve?
Have You forgotten to be gracious?
Have I wearied You?
Have I offended You?
Have You cast me off?
Where did I miss Your guidance?
When did I lose the way?
Do You see my utter despair?

You ask:
Are you trusting me?

Do not abandon me, Lord. Do not stand at a distance, my God. Come
quickly to help me, O Lord my savior. Psalm 38:21-22, NLT

October 3

I Have You

Sick depressed anxious

Fatigued frustrated

Puzzled perplexed lonely

Desperate despairing

Lord, for this I have You.

As for me, I am poor and needy, but the Lord is thinking about me right now. You are my helper and my savior. Do not delay, O my God.

Psalm 40:17, NLT

Big Switch

Once again I have utterly failed.

This time I thought I would make it.

I honestly thought I could cut it.

I thought it was all sewed up.

But here alone in my silent room

Your message rings loud and clear:

"Turn yourself in

And I will take over."

Could we make the Big Switch

Now, Lord?

The Lord is good. When trouble comes, he is a strong refuge. And he knows everyone who trusts in him.   Nahum 1:7, NLT

October 5

The Reason

Lord, we both know

I come to You

Boldly

Persistently

Expectantly

Day after day

Need after need

As if everything

In my entire life

Depended upon it.

There's a reason, Lord—

It does.

Blessed is he whose help is the God of Jacob, whose hope is in the
Lord his God, the Maker of heaven and earth, the sea, and everything
in them—the Lord, who remains faithful forever.   Psalm 146:5-6, NIV

Keep

I sit here at my desk
With Your Word before me—
A red pencil in my hand.
Suddenly the word *keep*
Looms from the page
Black and bold:
"He will *keep*
Keep
Keep
That which I have committed . . ."
Really, Lord?
This haunting anxiety?
This brick barrier which is
Blocking my peace?
This sinister intrusion?
It's so heavy, Lord
The weight of it is breaking me.
But You said You'd *keep*
So I give it to You now
Palms down.

Release!
Relief!
Laughter!
Joy!

And that is why I am suffering here in prison. But I am not ashamed
of it, for I know the one in whom I trust, and I am sure that he is able
to guard what I have entrusted to him until the day of his return.

2 Timothy 1:12, NLT

October 7

I Asked for a Sign

Even as I answer your letter, you are perhaps still waiting while God sends only silence. There is no sudden hailstorm, no writing in the sky. The crisis is real, and you don't want to be presumptuous. Like Gideon in Judges 6, you want to feel the wet fleece. Or the dry fleece—you don't care which one. You just want to *know!*

You don't stand alone! All of us who walk with God face conflicts that involve urgent decisions. God is not a God of confusion. We *can* know his will. When our faith is very new, he may send a sign to fortify us. However, I am convinced that God's highest intention is to free us from unnecessary "props." He wants to buttress us, not baby us. Above all, he wants us to trust his Word, not the wool! When he encourages us to hope in a promise, that hope may be our *only* evidence.

At this moment you can't see ahead. However, you can still be incorrigibly hopeful! You can anticipate as you wait, knowing that God will never disappoint the hope he himself implants. He is never too late. Remember: Not the wool but his Word!

Give your burdens to the Lord, and he will take care of you. He will not permit the godly to slip and fall. Psalm 55:22, NLT

You Wait for Me

Lord

I am so prone to

Extravagant extremes:

I either foolishly

Justify my imperfections

Or I frantically bemoan them.

All the while You wait for me

To release them—to You.

If we confess our sins, he is faithful and just and will forgive us our sins and purify us from all unrighteousness. If we claim we have not sinned, we make him out to be a liar and his word has no place in our lives.   1 John 1:9-10, NIV

October 9

Promotion

Dear God:

I resign.

Dear child:

Good!

Now I'll promote you.

Many are the plans in a man's heart, but it is the Lord's purpose
that prevails.
Proverbs 19:21, NIV

Beginning

Lord

I'm at the end

Of all my resources.

Child

You're just at the beginning

Of Mine.

Surely God is my help; the Lord is the one who sustains me.

Psalm 54:4, NIV

O c t o b e r 1 1

Failure

Sometimes, God

I feel like a failure

In everyone's sight but Yours.

Dear child

Be glad it isn't reversed.

You Love Me

Yesterday, God, I was soaring

Like a graceful eagle

And You loved me.

Today I feel like a blob

And You love me.

Tomorrow I may ask

"Whatever happened

To disturb me yesterday?"

And You'll love me.

God, there are innumerable things

I cannot begin to comprehend

But the one great certainty

In all my life is this:

I know that You love me.

For the Lord is good and his love endures forever; his faithfulness continues through all generations.   Psalm 100:5, NIV

October 13

I Will Let You

Early this morning, Lord
An hour or so before dawn
You whispered a secret
Within my trembling heart . . .

You said, "If you will let Me
I will make this seeming tragedy
The most valuable experience
Of your entire life.
I will blaze a luminous trail
Through the vast wilderness.
Where there is sand and tumbleweed
I will cultivate a fertile valley.
I will plant green trees by still waters.
If you will let Me."

O Lord, Yes!
I will let You!

Even the wilderness will rejoice in those days. The desert will blossom with flowers. Yes, there will be an abundance of flowers and singing and joy! The deserts will become as green as the mountains of Lebanon, as lovely as Mount Carmel's pastures and the plain of Sharon. There the Lord will display his glory, the splendor of our God.   Isaiah 35:1-2, NLT

October 14

The Lesson of the Windmill

Lorraine, Kansas, where I grew up, was known as the City of Windmills. I loved having one in our backyard. I was sure that if I climbed to the very top I could touch God! If only I was brave enough to try! My brother, two years younger than I, was usually eager to please me, so I begged him until he finally agreed. He stepped on the first rung, the second, the third and fourth.

"I'm proud of you!" I shouted.

Another rung . . . and another . . . and almost to the top. Then he looked down—and froze. Our mother heard his screams. When she saw her young son on the ladder, she calmly silenced his screams while I ran for our neighbor. In moments Johnnie was rescued. I knew he was angry. "You said if I climbed to the top I could touch God, but I didn't even see him."

Often God has used the memory of the windmill to remind me that we never reach God by climbing. Again and again we attempt to climb the rung of good works, the rung of prestige and success—until we discover anew that the *only* way to reach God is by kneeling at the foot of the Cross. He waits for us there!

It is by grace you have been saved, through faith—and this not from yourselves, it is the gift of God—not by works, so that no one can boast. Ephesians 2:8-9, NIV

October 15

The Time Is Now

O God

No temptation is irresistible.

I can absolutely trust You

To keep the temptation

From becoming so strong

That I can't stand against it.

You've promised this

And You will do what you say.

But I don't need the promise

For yesterday or tomorrow, Lord.

I need it today. Desperately.

This very moment.

Because he himself suffered when he was tempted, he is able to help those who are being tempted. Hebrews 2:18, NIV

October 16

Don't Stop, Lord

Lord

In asking You

To make me whole

I certainly didn't know

What I was in for.

You have ransacked me

Until I sometimes feel

There is nothing left.

But don't stop, Lord

Please don't stop!

I'm trusting that the product

Will be worth the process.

These trials are only to test your faith, to show that it is strong and pure. It is being tested as fire tests and purifies gold—and your faith is far more precious to God than mere gold. So if your faith remains strong after being tried by fiery trials, it will bring you much praise and glory and honor on the day when Jesus Christ is revealed to the whole world.

1 Peter 1:7, NLT

October 17

Patience

Lord, as I read Your Word today

I underlined these words:

"Don't be impatient for the Lord to act.

Keep traveling steadily along his pathway

And in due season he will honor you

With every blessing."

I know I need more patience, Lord

But I simply cannot create it.

I plead with You to do it for me.

And, Lord, could You hurry a little?

But when the Holy Spirit controls our lives, he will produce this kind of fruit in us: love, joy, peace, patience, kindness, goodness, faithfulness, gentleness, and self-control. Here there is no conflict with the law.

Galatians 5:22-23, NLT

October 18

Could You Hurry a Little

Lord, I know there are countless times
When I must wait patiently for You.
Waiting develops endurance.
It strengthens my faith
And deepens my dependence upon You.
I know You are Sovereign God—
Not an errand boy
Responding to the snap of my finger.
I know Your timing is neatly wrapped
In Your incomparable wisdom.
But, Lord
You have appointed prayer
To obtain answers!
Even David the Psalmist cried
With confident boldness:
"It is time, O Lord, for you to act."
God, on this silent sunless morning
When I am hedged in on every side
I too cry boldly.
You are my Father, and I am Your child.
So, Lord, could You hurry a little?

But you, O Lord, be not far off; O my Strength, come quickly
to help me.
Psalm 22:19, NIV

October 19

Only Goodness

What glorious words of wonder
Come from the Apostle Peter.
He wrote, "But we are looking forward
To God's promise of new heavens
And a new earth afterwards
Where there will be only goodness."

O dear God
"Where there will be only goodness."
After centuries of war, greed, and lust
After indulgences shamelessly practiced
After hatred, hostility
Jealousy and abuse.
Murder and martyrdom
Crime and cruelty
Curses and rebellion.
After whimpering cries from starving children
After tragedy and catastrophe
Loneliness and despair
At last . . . at long last
"There will be only goodness."
O dear Lord
Your promise is Your guarantee
But please hurry a little!

I heard a loud shout from the throne, saying, "Look, the home of God is now among his people! He will live with them, and they will be his people. God himself will be with them. He will remove all of their sorrows, and there will be no more death or sorrow or crying or pain. For the old world and its evils are gone forever." Revelation 21:3-4, NLT

October 20

Autumn Glow

Lord, if You will make

The autumn of my life

As lovely as this

Golden autumn morning

I will not look back to grieve

The passing days of summer.

Of all the regal seasons

Autumn is most brilliant.

Make my life brilliant, too!

But I trust in you, O Lord; I say, "You are my God." My times are
in your hands. Psalm 31:14-15, NIV

October 21

Nobody Can Possibly Help Me

How wonderful! You can shake hands with a king. His name is Jehoshaphat, and his story reads like a letter from someone who feels desperate—maybe like you feel right now. You don't know where to turn. Neither did he. Jehoshaphat had no forces to oppose the "great company" marching against him.

Standing achingly helpless (as you are), what did he do? He literally threw himself on God. He prayed, "O our God, we have no power to face this vast army attacking us. We don't know what to do, but our eyes are upon you." (You'll find the story in 2 Chronicles 20.)

Do you see yourself in the mirror of the story? Do you feel overpowered by a "great company" of temptations. Are you stumbling through confused days and tossing through sleepless nights.

What is the answer? Stoic endurance? No. That brings only deeper despair. But you *can* pray Jehoshaphat's prayer! His God is your God if your faith is in Jesus Christ. You can plead with God on the grounds of his great power, his promises, and his love. And all the while *you can keep your eyes steadfastly on him.*

The result? As you trust, you will one day say as Jehoshaphat said, "The Lord has given me cause to rejoice."

"O Lord, God of our fathers, are you not the God who is in heaven? You rule over all the kingdoms of the nations. Power and might are in your hand, and no one can withstand you. . . . O our God . . . We do not know what to do, but our eyes are upon you."

2 Chronicles 20:6, 12, NIV

I Shout for Joy

Sometimes, Lord

You seem a million miles away

And then I remember Your unfailing words:

"I will never, never let go of your hand."

Once again I shout for joy

That what *seems* to be

Is not always what is.

Come, everyone, and clap your hands for joy! Shout to God with joyful praise! For the Lord Most High is awesome. He is the great King of all the earth.   Psalm 47:1-2, NLT

October 23

The Hardest Thing

O God
In these crisis days
Of piercing pain
And emotional fatigue
Do a brand new thing in me.
Give me water in the wilderness
And streams in my desert.
You have promised to be my God
Through all my lifetime.
Surely You will keep Your word!

As You promised
Give me rest from my sorrow
And from my fear
And from the bondage
That binds me.
One thing more, dear Lord:
Enable me to praise You
When to praise
Is the hardest thing of all.

Then maidens will dance and be glad, young men and old as well. I
will turn their mourning into gladness; I will give them comfort and
joy instead of sorrow.   Jeremiah 31:13, NIV

Soundproof

God of penitent hearts

The moment Your prophet Isaiah

Knew You had cleansed his sin

At that very moment

He heard Your Voice

Addressed directly to him.

Lord, thank You

For the revealing discovery

That only one thing

Makes me soundproof

Against Your Voice:

My refusal to relinquish my sin.

Then I said, "My destruction is sealed, for I am a sinful man and a member of a sinful race. Yet I have seen the King, the Lord Almighty!"

Isaiah 6:5, NLT

The Pain of Growth

O God
Growth is a painful process.
I frankly confess
I am a coward about pain.
I don't like it, Lord.
I never pray for it
Or get excited over it.
In fact, I often resist it:
The pain of emotional trauma
So overwhelming
So baffling and crushing.
The deep-cutting pain
Of a broken relationship.
Physical pain that goes on and on
Until my entire body screams.
The pain of cruel cutting words.
The pain of loneliness, rejection
Or financial ruin.

The pain of being misunderstood.
Lord, the very thought of pain
Frightens and unnerves me.
Yet it is true—
Again and again it is true:
My greatest spiritual growth
Has come through pain.
Through heartache
And anguish.
And very often in my suffering
When I sadly thought
You were doing absolutely nothing
At that very moment
You were doing more *within* me
Than I ever dreamed or hoped.

I know, O Lord, that your laws are righteous, and in faithfulness you
have afflicted me. May your unfailing love be my comfort, according
to your promise to your servant.   Psalm 119:75-76, NIV

October 26

My Glorious Enough

Oh, how I love You, my Lord

But not enough.

How I hunger and thirst for You

But not enough.

How I rejoice in Your inimitable goodness

But not enough.

Pour Yourself lavishly, dear God

Into every vacant hollow

Into every cluttered chamber

Of my longing heart.

Free me from every shallow substitute

From every hidden pretense

Until I shall know

With deep, consuming conviction

That You are my Glorious Enough.

Blessed are those who hunger and thirst for righteousness, for they will be filled.

Matthew 5:6, NIV

October 27

I Am Sure of You

Lord, I was sure of my faith

Just long enough

To watch it collapse.

Now I am sure of *You*

And You will not collapse.

The name of the Lord is a strong fortress; the godly run to him and are safe.

Proverbs 18:10, NLT

October 28

I Do Know

There is much I cannot begin to fathom concerning the vast, indescribable universe created by our majestic God. There is much I will never comprehend. I want to sing and shout, so utterly overwhelmed I am with the magnitude of God.

But I do know with confident certainty that I belong to the God of the universe—the Creator of all that exists. I know that I, a mere mortal, am forever linked to divine destiny. I know that my life has purpose and dignity. I know that God has chosen me as the object of his lavish love; that his thoughts toward me are thoughts of kindness and mercy; that he has inscribed me in the palms of his hands. I know that all the love of the Father, and the life of the Son, and the power of the Holy Spirit are freely, inseparably mine—now and throughout all eternity.

This I do *know!*

I know the one in whom I trust, and I am sure that he is able to guard what I have entrusted to him until the day of his return.

2 Timothy 1:12, NLT

October 29

Nevertheless

Lord, right now

My life is one gigantic puzzle.

None of the pieces fit together.

None of them, Lord!

In my stupor and confusion

I confess I don't understand Your hand.

Nevertheless, My child

You can always trust My heart.

O Sovereign Lord, you are God! Your words are trustworthy, and you have promised these good things to your servant.   2 Samuel 7:28, NIV

Unexplainable Mystery

Mysterious God
Today I am desolate
I am puzzled
I am heartsick
That I must wait so long
When You have promised so much.
At the same time
I am conscience-stricken
That I should feel such bitter rebellion.
Yet, to try to hide my emotions
Would only build up a pretense
That would eventually be exposed.
I suppose, O God
In the great perplexities
Of my unpredictable life
One of two things will always happen:
Either I will crowd You out
(Slowly but surely)
Or I will acknowledge Your sovereignty
In every area of my bewildered life.
To offer myself to You
Regardless of circumstances
May always bring unexplainable mystery.
But rejecting You totally
Brings the depth of despair.

May my cry come before you, O Lord; give me understanding
according to your word. May my supplication come before you; deliver
me according to your promise.   Psalm 119:169-170, NIV

October 31

Enormous Rewards

O dear God

Thank You for teaching me

The enormous rewards

Of walking obediently with You:

There is joy without guilt

Freedom without fear

Satisfaction without sordidness

Purpose without confusion

Friendship without compromise

Forgiveness without penance

Fulfillment without disappointment.

Now to him who is able to do immeasurably more than all we ask or imagine, according to his power that is at work within us, to him be glory in the church and in Christ Jesus throughout all generations, for ever and ever! Amen. *Ephesians 3:20, NIV*

November

The Promise of Help

When I finally confess my inability to make it alone,

God whispers, "That's why you have me!"

God is my helper. The Lord is the one who keeps me
alive!   Psalm 54:4, NLT

Worst—Best

O God

It is difficult for me to think coherently

To pray with any kind of sequence today.

I am so weary, so worn, so fragmented.

But, Lord, perhaps to Your ears

Sometimes my worst praying

Is really my best.

I trust so . . . I trust so.

One thing I do know:

All my desire is before You!

And the Holy Spirit helps us in our distress. For we don't even know what we should pray for, nor how we should pray. But the Holy Spirit prays for us with groanings that cannot be expressed in words. And the Father who knows all hearts knows what the Spirit is saying, for the Spirit pleads for us believers in harmony with God's own will.

Romans 8:26-27, NLT

Busy Day

Lord, this is one of the days
I must ask You to preserve my sanity
In the midst of turmoil.
I'm so pressed by commitments—
Plus a thousand trivial tasks—
That I can scarcely see over my head.
So I plead for enough wisdom
To sort my priorities carefully.
Regardless of my frenzied schedule
May I keep my sense of humor
And even enjoy a hearty chuckle or two.

Calm my quivering nerves
With mental flashes from Your Word.
Help me to maintain
At least a semblance
Of Mary-Martha balance.
And tonight when we're together again
Should my husband confront me with
"What have you been doing today?"
May my answer be genuine and gentle:
"Part of the time, darling
I've thanked God for you."

But the Lord said to her, "My dear Martha, you are so upset over all these details!"
Luke 10:41, NLT

Feeling Spiritual

Lord, I keep remembering
Our happy time last night—
Just You and me
In the quiet of our family room.
I had been reading a devotional book
Very "spiritual"
Very inspirational
So challenging
I doubted that I'd ever reach the goal.
Suddenly the book felt heavy
Sentences twirled
Words collided
And with all my valiant effort
I simply could not feel "spiritual."
Then, glancing at a Charlie Brown book
I thought I heard You say
"Let's read it together—
You and me."
I was delighted.
We read and laughed
And read and laughed . . .
And just as we finished the last page
You said what I needed most to hear:
"Never worry about feeling 'spiritual.'
Just share *everything* with me."

Now the Lord is the Spirit, and where the Spirit of the Lord is,
there is freedom.
2 Corinthians 3:17, NIV

Lord, You Love to Say Yes

Lord, I asked You for abundant life
Rich, challenging, full of adventure
And You said Yes.
I asked You for an undisturbable joy
Independent of transitory change
And You said Yes.
I asked You to thread my tears into a song
When I was shattered and torn with grief
And You said Yes.
I asked You to steady me when I staggered—
To hold me when I struggled
To seize me when I resisted
And You said Yes.
I asked You to forgive my vain grasping
My foolish fears, my willful pride
And You said Yes.
I asked You to be my Helper, my Friend
My Light in the darkness
And You said Yes.
I asked You to guide me all my life
With Your wisdom, Your counsel
Your captivating love
And You said Yes.
Sometimes, Lord
I feel like a spoiled child
Who gets whatever he asks for.
You overwhelm me with joy
For *You love to say Yes!*

He fills my life with good things. My youth is renewed like the
eagle's!   Psalm 103:5, NLT

November 5

Romans 8——to Me

God
I may fall flat on my face
I may fail until I feel
Old and beaten and done in
Yet Your love for me is changeless.
All the music may go out of my
    life
My private world may shatter to
    dust
Even so You will hold me
In the palm of Your steady hand.
No turn in the affairs
Of my fractured life
Can baffle You.
Satan with all his braggadocio
Cannot distract You.
Nothing can separate me
From Your measureless love:

Pain can't
Disappointments can't
Anguish can't.
Yesterday, today, tomorrow can't.
The loss of my dearest love can't.

Death can't.
Life can't.
Riots war insanity unidentity
Hunger neurosis disease—
None of these things
Nor all of them heaped together
Can budge the fact
That I am dearly loved.
Completely forgiven
And forever free
Through Jesus Christ
Your beloved Son.

And I am convinced that nothing can ever separate us from his love.
Death can't, and life can't. The angels can't, and the demons can't.
Our fears for today, our worries about tomorrow, and even the powers
of hell can't keep God's love away. Whether we are high above the sky
or in the deepest ocean, nothing in all creation will ever be able to
separate us from the love of God that is revealed in Christ Jesus our
Lord.   Romans 8:38-39, NLT

November 6

Last Word

I read, "In everything give thanks."
I said, "Lord, I'm in deep trouble—
You know I can't thank You for this."
You said, "My word is a command
And not a suggestion, dear child."

I read, "Your sins are forgiven you."
I said, "Thank you for forgiving me—
I repeat the same sin so often."
You said, "I can deliver, as well as forgive."

I read, "Trust in the Lord at all times."
I said, "You know how earnestly I try."
You said, "My Word says Trust."

Lord, it seems to me
You always have
The last word.

For the word of God is full of living power. It is sharper than the sharpest knife, cutting deep into our innermost thoughts and desires. It exposes us for what we really are.   Hebrews 4:12, NLT

November 7

Discipline

It was a chilly morning. The warm blankets felt wonderful. After a two-minute struggle, I surrendered. In less than a minute I was asleep again.

For weeks I had been getting up at six o'clock. With my Bible and my journal I had spent uninterrupted time with God. The spiritual value far surpassed the discomfort of a cold morning. Why had I disrupted the habit? God wasn't shaking his finger, but why had I cheated myself?

Not wanting to miss out entirely, I opened my Bible to the book of Proverbs. One verse held my attention:

> I will teach you wisdom's ways and lead you in straight paths. (Proverbs 4:11)

Later in the day as I glanced out the window I saw her: Our eighty-year-old neighbor taking her three-mile walk. Rain or shine she walked.

One day I finally asked, "Kay, is it hard for you to walk three miles every day?"

"It's *very* hard," she said. "But not nearly as hard on my disposition as being undisciplined!"

Clearly I saw it! The purpose of discipline is to *free* us, not to enslave us.

Cry out for insight and understanding. Search for them as you would for lost money or hidden treasure. Then you will understand what it means to fear the Lord, and you will gain knowledge of God.

Proverbs 2:3-5, NLT

Reversal

Lord

For so long

I thought Your love

Demanded that I change.

At last

I am beginning to understand

That Your love

Changes me.

God demonstrates his own love for us in this: While we were still sinners, Christ died for us.

Romans 5:8, NIV

Celebration

When I think of Your lavish goodness
The longings You've satisfied
The forgiveness You've granted
The promises You've kept
When I think of Your irresistible love
Your ceaseless care
Your unfailing protection . . .

O Lord God
I want to raise flags
And fly banners
And sound bugles.
I want to run with lighted torches
And praise You
From the mountaintop.
I want to write symphonies
And shout for joy.
I want to throw a festive party
For ten thousand guests.
I want to celebrate with streamers
And bright lights
And an elaborate banquet.

Fine, dear child.
I'm ready.

I will exalt you, my God the King; I will praise your name for ever
and ever. Every day I will praise you and extol your name for ever
and ever.   Psalm 145:1-2, NIV

November 10

Just Cry

Lord, the sky is black and ominous

And all sense of Your presence is gone.

I am utterly devoid of energy

I am thwarted at every turn

My fragmented thoughts

Refuse to form words

All I can bring to You

Is my anguished cry.

Then cry, dear child

Just cry.

I cry aloud to the Lord; I lift up my voice to the Lord for mercy.
I pour out my complaint before him; before him I tell my trouble.

Psalm 142:1-2, NIV

The Reason

God, why am I so often defeated?

Why am I so full of dread and anxiety?

Why am I so lamentably weak—

So perilously susceptible to temptation?

Why am I often inhospitable

So intolerant of the needs of others?

Why am I so undisciplined

So restless and dissatisfied?

Why do I protest so violently?

Above all, God

Why do I so frequently lose

The sense of Your shining Presence?

God, why?

Why?

Because you pray so little.

Keep on praying.   1 Thessalonians 5:17, NLT

Too Sleepy

When I awoke this morning

You said so clearly

"Don't worry about anything

Instead, pray about everything . . ."

So, dear Lord, all day long

Will You keep me so prayerfully occupied

With Your assigned tasks

That I will find no time to worry?

Then tonight, when I finally lie down

And stretch out on my comfortable bed

Please silence my clamoring thoughts

And make me too sleepy to worry.

Do not be anxious about anything, but in everything, by prayer and petition, with thanksgiving, present your requests to God. And the peace of God, which transcends all understanding, will guard your hearts and your minds in Christ Jesus. Philippians 4:6-7, NIV

November 13

I Try

Lord

Never in a million years

Could I adequately thank You

For Your amazing goodness

Your matchless love—

But I like to try!

I will give thanks to the Lord because of his righteousness and will
sing praise to the name of the Lord Most High. Psalm 7:17, NIV

November 14

It Happened to Me

It may be a question you'd rather not face. You've struggled with it for so long. A resentment, perhaps, or a seething rebellion . . . or an ugly jealousy that keeps churning. There may be someone you haven't forgiven, despite a whole string of resolutions. Day after day, in fact week after week, you live with no sense of fulfillment, no recharge of joy, no happy expectations. You long for a deeper understanding of God's will for your life. Your heart feels empty, your soul feels weary.

Do you wonder if there is a way out? If other Christians have found the secret? Oh, yes! Assuredly YES! Let me tell you *when!* When they were *desperate* enough to trust the Holy Spirit to do what they could not do. When they were *simple* enough to trust God's promise: "I will put my Spirit within you." When they were *willing* enough to open their hearts and give it all over to God.

Do you wonder why I am so joyfully sure? *It happened to me!*

I will give you a new heart with new and right desires, and I will put a new spirit in you. I will take out your stony heart of sin and give you a new, obedient heart. Ezekiel 36:26, NLT

I Praise You

I praise You, my Lord!

I praise You for all things:

For this very moment

For future days

For the past

Often so reckless

On my part

So filled with

Foolish fantasies.

But so gracious

On Your part

So loving

And so totally forgiving.

I praise You!

I will praise you, my God and King, and bless your name forever
and ever. I will bless you every day, and I will praise you forever.

Psalm 145:1-2, NLT

Wrong Center

Lord, I'm so discouraged.

Again and again I've struggled

To get hold of myself

But I simply can't do it.

Weary child

Your center is wrong.

The secret is—

Get hold of Me.

I wait quietly before God, for my salvation comes from him. He alone is my rock and my salvation, my fortress where I will never be shaken.

Psalm 62:1-2, NLT

Not Tomorrow

Lord

You have promised forgiveness

To my sincere repentance.

With all my heart

I praise You for that.

But may I never reject

The unalterable truth

That You have not promised tomorrow

To my procrastination.

A lazy person sleeps soundly—and goes hungry.   Proverbs 19:15, NLT

November 18

Release

You are showing me, Lord

That when I cling to negative thoughts

Regarding the actions of my family

I thwart Your divine purpose

And turn their actions upon myself.

I am beginning to grasp

That I must *release* to You

What I too often *resent* in others.

If you forgive those who sin against you, your heavenly Father will
forgive you. But if you refuse to forgive others, your Father will not
forgive your sins.
Matthew 6:14-15, NLT

Unnecessary

How patiently You wait, dear God

Until having battered myself

Against the impregnable wall

Of my own selfishness and rebellion

I turn at last

Broken and bruised

Into Your wide-open arms.

It is then that I learn

That all my struggling, my panic

My foolish pretenses were unnecessary—

Had I simply fallen trustingly

Into Your waiting arms

At the very beginning.

Even youths grow tired and weary, and young men stumble and fall; but those who hope in the Lord will renew their strength. They will soar on wings like eagles; they will run and not grow weary, they will walk and not be faint.

Isaiah 40:30-31, NIV

Turnabout

God, for so long
I thought that by praying
I could change Your mind.
Often I prayed
Fervently, pleadingly
Until I felt
Emotionally pulverized.
Then I gradually began to grasp
That the purpose of prayer
Is to find *Your* mind
And let You change mine.
Little by little
The turnabout is renewing me.
Slowly I begin to feel
A settling quietness.
I wait while You woo me
To Your will, dear Lord.
I wait until my thoughts
Harmonize with Yours.
For in my deepest heart
Despite my guarded resistance
I somehow sense
That what You want for me
Is stupendously more
Than anything I could
Dream or wish or want
For myself.

Search me, O God, and know my heart; test me and know my anxious thoughts. See if there is any offensive way in me, and lead me in the way everlasting.
                                                    Psalm 139:23-24, NIV

November 21

The "Someday" Syndrome

The "Someday" Syndrome! How prevalent it has become in our "advanced" society. How thought-consuming; how time-consuming. "Someday" when we've bought a bigger house, when we've installed our swimming pool, when we've taken another trip or two . . .

"Someday" we'll be able to give more to the hungry, to the needy. But right now there are so many pressing demands, so many social events that consume both time and money. "Someday" the struggle will be less taxing.

However, it doesn't really work that way. "Someday" never seems to happen. It's only when giving becomes primary and getting becomes secondary that we begin to see things from God's point of view.

When we obey God's Word, his giving never stops. We need to be spiritually prepared to catch his gifts!

If you give, you will receive. Your gift will return to you in full measure, pressed down, shaken together to make room for more, and running over. Whatever measure you use in giving—large or small— it will be used to measure what is given back to you.   Luke 6:38, NLT

November 22

Suddenly or Finally

Right now, dear God

In my bewildering day of turmoil

I call upon You

With unashamed boldness.

I come to You directly

Before seeking out family or friends.

You have promised to extricate me

According to Your infallible Word.

I offer You now my sacrifice of praise

For I know my deliverance will come.

"He is faithful that promised."

And, dear Lord, when You do deliver me

Whether it be suddenly or finally

I pledge my continual gratitude.

In fact, You'll never hear the end of it!

Let us hold unswervingly to the hope we profess, for he who promised is faithful.

Hebrews 10:23, NIV

Thanksgiving Day Dream

On this fragrant, frosty Thanksgiving Day
The huge turkey browns beautifully
In our king-size oven.
The tender yams are evenly candied;
The corn soufflé is beginning to bubble;
The congealed salad is ready to unmold.
The homemade bread with its crunchy texture
Is wrapped in foil for reheating.
The ice cubes are bagged in plastic;
The relishes are artistically arranged
On a round crystal plate.
The pumpkin pies are still slightly warm.
Fresh yellow chrysanthemums
Grace the long, colorful table.
The house glistens and shines.
My makeup is evenly applied. . . .

So, dear family
How about settling down
In our favorite chairs
For an hour of relaxation
Before our guests arrive!

Lord, I dream of this happening
Some ethereal Thanksgiving Day!

Then the King will say to those on the right, "Come, you who are
blessed by my Father, inherit the Kingdom prepared for you from
the foundation of the world. For I was hungry, and you fed me. I was
thirsty, and you gave me a drink. I was a stranger, and you invited me
into your home."
Matthew 25:34-35, NLT

Disciplined One

Today I promised myself
I wouldn't eat a bite of candy—
Not a single bite.
I kept that promise.
I promised myself
I'd walk two miles
And I walked almost three.
I kept that promise.
I promised myself
I'd clean the messy refrigerator.
I kept that promise.
I promised myself
I'd read a magazine article
About choosing priorities.
I kept that promise.
I promised myself
There would be no bedtime snack.
I cheated. I failed.
I just couldn't resist
Those crackers with the tangy
    cheese.
(At least I *didn't* resist.)

Well, four out of five promises
    kept—
That's at least better than yesterday.

O Lord
I struggle so with discipline!
Sometimes the very word
    depresses me.
Nevertheless, keep turning me
Toward the right direction.
Even though a detour from time
    to time
Doesn't mean total defeat
I do so long for the rugged
    strength
That discipline always builds.
Forcefully remind me, dear God
That unbridled behavior
Always leads to discontent.
I really want to follow You, Lord
And a disciple is a disciplined
    one!

But since we belong to the day, let us be self-controlled, putting on
faith and love as a breastplate, and the hope of salvation as a helmet.

1 Thessalonians 5:8, NIV

November 25

There Are No Words

How can I put into words, my Lord

The flooding, transforming power

That sweeps my life because of You?

How can I explain to anyone

The soaring, surging peace

That You alone can give?

All the wonder-filled things in my life

All the joyful, glorious things

I owe to Your goodness, Your grace, Your love.

Nothing is ever the same since knowing You

And the longer I know You

The deeper my love.

Now, our God, we give you thanks, and praise your glorious name.

1 Chronicles 29:13, NIV

November 26

Thanksgiving Morning

Early on Thanksgiving morning
Before my family awakened
I began to form a list entitled
Reasons for Gratitude.
Then, halfway down the page
I pensively wondered—
Lord, do I give You any reasons
To be thankful for me?

Give thanks to the Lord, for he is good; his love endures forever.

Psalm 118:1, NIV

Dead Giveaway

O dear God

My heart overflows

With proclamations of joy!

You are so good

So faithful

Your loving-kindness is so great.

I long for my continual gratitude

To be a dead giveaway

Of my deepening love for You.

I will thank you, Lord, with all my heart; I will tell of all the
marvelous things you have done. I will be filled with joy because
of you. I will sing praises to your name, O Most High.

Psalm 9:1-2, NLT

November 28

Fiery Trials

God is teaching me incredible lessons regarding growth. I see with undeniable evidence that growth means pruning, and pruning means pain. I confess, I'm actually a coward about pain. I certainly never pray for it. I don't anticipate or look for it. I do only one thing. I ask God to steady me, since the Bible so clearly states that trials are a part of our lifewalk with him.

In all honesty I would prefer to escape the testing. I don't like the pain of emotional trauma, which can be so overwhelming and baffling. I don't like the deep cutting pain that goes on and on without relief. The pain of loneliness frightens me, the pain of losing someone dear to me grieves me.

Nevertheless, I am praying for an open heart. I can't begin to contemplate what fiery ordeals God may choose for my testing and growth, but I do long for my *yieldedness* to prove my *willingness* to be conformed to the image of his dear Son.

Dear friends, don't be surprised at the fiery trials you are going through, as if something strange were happening to you.

1 Peter 4:12, NLT

The Deliberate No

O God, teach me to say
The deliberate and releasing word *no*
Without a spiritual tug-of-war
Between variations of false guilt.
May I say it tactfully
Kindly and gently
But enable me to *say* it!
If on occasions I am forced
To confront an honest doubt
May I wait patiently
For Your clear guidance.
May this powerful truth
Penetrate the inner chambers of my being:
It is better to say a God-guided no
Than a self-guided yes.
Lord, remind me often
That a squirrel cage
Can be mighty confining.
So can a heart attack
And a hospital bed.

So now there is no condemnation for those who belong to Christ
Jesus. For the power of the life-giving Spirit has freed you through
Christ Jesus from the power of sin that leads to death.

Romans 8:1-2, NLT

November 30

Renewed Commitment

Forgive me, dear Lord
For too often
Letting the painful memories
Of my yesterdays
Crowd out the glad tomorrows
You graciously offer me.
I know I cannot rekindle
The charred embers
Of the past year.
I cannot erase the blunders
Made so impulsively
Nor can I regain the opportunities
That are forever lost.
I cannot retract the impetuous words
I wish I had not spoken
Or replace the shallow choices
I should not have made.
But I *can* open my wayward heart
To Your cleansing power.
With honest determination
I *can* renew my broken vows.
And I *can* begin to praise You
This very day
For the joy of beginning again.

You turned my wailing into dancing; you removed my sackcloth and
clothed me with joy, that my heart may sing to you and not be silent.

Psalm 30:11-12, NIV

December

The Promise of Belonging

Home for Christmas!

Home to look with swelling gratitude into

the loving face of the Savior who came

to make his home in our hearts.

Home for Christmas because of him!

[If] you belong to Christ, you are . . . his heirs, and now
all the promises God gave to him belong to you.

Galatians 3:29, NLT

The Gift

It's Christmas, Lord
It's Your birthday.
What can I give You—
You who have given
So much to me?
I search and search
Through my talents
My possessions
My friendships
My loves
But with all my searching
I find nothing new.
Strangely—
Whatever I could offer
Is always that
Which You have first
Given me.
And now in the soft silence
I hear You say
What I want from you—
Is you.

See how very much our heavenly Father loves us, for he allows us
to be called his children, and we really are!   1 John 3:1, NLT

Christmas

The stable—my heart

The guiding star—Your perfect plan

The Song—"Just As I Am"

The gift—my irrevocable Yes

The joy—Your immeasurable love

The hope—the King is coming

Lord, this is my personal paraphrase

Of Christmas.

Long live the king! May the gold of Sheba be given to him.

Psalm 72:15, NLT

December 3

A Better Way

Lord, I'm utterly exhausted
From standing on tiptoe
Shouting my numerous wants.
My lips are dry
My eyes burn
My muscles ache
My nerves are tense.
I'm beginning to wonder
If it would be better
For me to relax
While You lean down
And whisper to me.

And after the earthquake there was a fire, but the Lord was not in
the fire. And after the fire there was the sound of a gentle whisper.
When Elijah heard it, he wrapped his face in his cloak and went out
and stood at the entrance of the cave. And a voice said, "What are
you doing here, Elijah?"
                                        1 Kings 19:12-13, NLT

December 4

Forever Worthy

Dear God
I have sinned
Against Heaven
And against You.
I am no longer worthy
To be called Your child.

Child, I know . . . I know . . .
But My Son
Is forever worthy
To be called your Savior.

We had to celebrate this happy day. For your brother was dead
and has come back to life! He was lost, but now he is found!

Luke 15:32, NLT

December 5

Reversal

I said: Lord, look at me
Just look at me
All of life upside down—
Tangled emotions smeared with
    fear
Guilt
Despair
Disgust
A prisoner of myself.
The hopeless thing is that
It's all decided.
I'm defenseless
At the end of my rope
Locked in
And I've tried, Lord
Tried desperately.
But how does one see without eyes
Or walk without feet?
How, Lord?

You said: Come unto Me.
You need not cringe
Nor climb
Nor compete
Nor change
Come even without feeling
Without tokens
Without merit or hope

But come.
Come now.
I came
And all of life
Turned right side up.

In my anguish I cried to the Lord, and he answered by setting me free.

Psalm 118:5, NIV

December 6

The Time Is Now

Lord

I see with startling clarity

That life is never long enough

To put You off

Until tomorrow.

The things that are before

Are all too soon behind.

I can never pick up

The years I've put down.

If I intend

To walk with You tomorrow

I must start today.

Another said, "Yes, Lord, I will follow you, but first let me say good-bye to my family." But Jesus told him, "Anyone who puts a hand to the plow and then looks back is not fit for the Kingdom of God."

Luke 9:61-62, NLT

December 7

The Man God Honors

There are thousands of men in the world. Men come in assorted sizes—tall and short, wide and lean. There are bankers, salesmen, politicians, mechanics, lawyers, teachers. But the man God honors is marked by at least five characteristics:

FIRST: He is a man totally committed to God, and his concern is that he will obey God's Word, whatever the cost.

SECOND: He is a man whose faith can be defined as confident trust. His high priority is prayer, knowing that a supernatural God works in supernatural ways.

THIRD: He rests his past, present, and future in the hands of an all-loving God, even in times of turbulence, uncertainty, agony, misunderstanding, and pain, assured that his times are in God's hands.

FOURTH: He believes with all his heart that, as he keeps steadily traveling along God's pathway, God will honor him with every blessing.

FIFTH: He has one consistent desire: "God, make me a man after your own heart."

Oh, the joys of those who do not follow the advice of the wicked, or stand around with sinners, or join in with scoffers. But they delight in doing everything the Lord wants; day and night they think about his law.

Psalm 1:1-2, NLT

December 8

Now

Lord
I don't ask You to renovate me
Nor do I ask You to reconstruct me
Or make me over.
I don't even ask You to patch me up
Or pare out the bruised spots
Or gloss over the tin and tarnish.
Rather, dear Lord, I ask You
To make a new species—
Something that never before existed.
Impart to me Your very own Life.
After all, Lord
It is such a simple thing for You
To create something beautiful
From a shapeless, chaotic mass.
It is such a simple thing for You
To divide light from darkness.
Please do it for me—now.

Child of My Infinite Plan
Two thousand years ago
All you have asked I did.
Please accept it from Me—now.

Therefore, if anyone is in Christ, he is a new creation; the old has gone, the new has come!

2 Corinthians 5:17, NIV

December 9

Gift Exchange

Dear God

This Christmas

I want to give You me.

I come just as I am

Unboxed

Unribboned

Without glitter

Or glamour.

On the name tag of my heart

I've written

"To God with love."

Do with me exactly as you choose.

Dear child
I choose to give you Me.

To him who loves us and has freed us from our sins by his blood,
and has made us to be a kingdom and priests to serve his God and
Father—to him be glory and power for ever and ever! Amen.

Revelation 1:5-6, NIV

I Will Be Pleased

Lord, this fresh early morning
As I sit in our quiet living room
You've just reminded me
Through David the Psalmist
That there is incomparable joy
For those who delight to please You—
For those who are thinking about ways
To follow You more closely.
Lord, the day stretches out before me.
In a few brief moments I must arouse my family
And face again the noise, the distraction
The hubbub of confusion.
But while we are still alone
Just the two of us, my Lord
While Your peace floods my tranquil heart
Please tell me what I can do
This duty-packed day
To follow You more closely.

Dearly loved child
Praise me joyfully
Talk with me intimately
Trust me totally
And I will be pleased.

Blessed are those who have learned to acclaim you, who walk in the
light of your presence, O Lord.   Psalm 89:15, NIV

An Echo

God, may I never be content

To be but the echo

Of my environment.

Empower me day by day

To be the echo

Of Your amazing love

In my God-guarded life!

But thanks be to God, who made us his captives and leads us along in Christ's triumphal procession. Now wherever we go he uses us to tell others about the Lord and to spread the Good News like a sweet perfume. 2 Corinthians 2:14, NLT

You Cannot Be Hid

Lord, I've discovered it's never a secret

When You live in a home

For You simply cannot be hid.

The neighbors soon know You are there

Even strangers learn of Your presence.

When You are the Great First in a home

There is a radiance that speaks of joy

There is gentleness, kindness

Laughter and love.

There is commotion mixed with contentment

There are problems mixed with prayer.

Lord, Your own Word says it so vividly:

"It was known that He was in the house."

You are the light of the world—like a city on a mountain, glowing in
the night for all to see. Don't hide your light under a basket! Instead,
put it on a stand and let it shine for all.　　　　Matthew 5:14-15, NLT

December 13

Book of All Books

Lord, I am overwhelmed
As I read Your living Word.
What power, what pungency
I find within its pages.
It stirs me, burns within me
It challenges me, invigorates me
And often disturbs me.
When I obey its commands
The results are what You claim:
Darkness becomes light
Crooked places become straight
The more I seek, the more I find.
Within its pages, God
I see beyond mere philosophy
I see beyond a neat package of ethics.
I crash head-on with a living Person
The One who makes all things new.
No other book can claim as much.

The word of God is living and active. Sharper than any two-edged
sword, it penetrates even to dividing soul and spirit, joints and
marrow; it judges the thoughts and attitudes of the heart.

Hebrews 4:12, NIV

Haunted House

When I opened the door to my young friend, I knew she had been crying. She carried a small suitcase, and before I could invite her in she said, "I'm coming to live with you."

As we sat at the kitchen table drinking hot chocolate, she repeated the story of her dysfunctional home. She had shared it often before. I ached for her, yet I felt so helpless. After an hour I said, "Now I must call your mother. She'll be worried about you. I'm sure she wants you to come home."

Again the tears and stumbling words: "I don't live in a home. I live in a haunted house."

My friend is an adult now, making her way in the world as best she can. But I never think of her without remembering that throughout our vast nation there are countless families who live in "haunted houses." Houses haunted by bitterness, rebellion, alcohol, and drugs . . . haunted by disgraceful abuse and neglect.

There is *no* substitute for an authentic home. A home where character and values and love and laughter add joy to living. A home where God is invited to live. God longs to empower us to remake what we have allowed the adversary to break!

Choose today whom you will serve. . . . As for me and my family, we will serve the Lord.

Joshua 24:15, NLT

The Most—The Least

Lord, when I feel exuberant
Bursting with energy and strength
When everything in my life
Seems to be going amazingly well
Then, dear God
I think I can accomplish anything for You.
In fact, *everything*.
I'm ready to go for it!
But when pain and depression grab me
And trials clobber me unmercifully
When I am hurt by criticism
Or neglected by my family
Or burdened with numerous demands
Then I am convinced
I can serve You in no way at all.

Often, dear child
When you think
You are doing the most
You are serving the least.
And when you think
You are doing the least
As you rest in my love
You are serving Me best.

"Why are you crying?" Jesus asked her. "Who are you looking for?"
She thought he was the gardener. "Sir," she said, "if you have taken
him away, tell me where you have put him, and I will go and get him."
"Mary!" Jesus said. She turned toward him and exclaimed,
"Teacher!"

John 20:15-16, NLT

December 16

I Cannot Imagine

God of my pensive heart

I cannot imagine

A day without the dawn

Or the sky without a star

Or a bird without a song

Or my life without You.

December 17

Slow Growth

In my fretful impatience
I am so often inclined to ask
"Why can't she change?"
"Why is he always so slow?"
"Will they ever learn from past mistakes?"
And then You begin to impress me
With my own slow progress upward.
I see Your stretched-out patience.
I remember how long You've waited for me.
And I grieve that my attitude
Is so often intolerant.
O God, keep fresh the imprint
Of my own need to grow
And make me more flexible
More understanding
And always more loving.

Be kind and compassionate to one another, forgiving each other, just as in Christ God forgave you.

Ephesians 4:32, NIV

December 18

In the End

God, it is not always easy

To know and do Your will.

But of this I am wholly convinced:

In the end, nothing else matters.

He went on a little farther and fell face down on the ground, praying, "My Father! If it is possible, let this cup of suffering be taken away from me. Yet I want your will, not mine." Matthew 26:39, NLT

December 19

You Show Yourself Strong

Dear Lord, Your Word says
Your eyes search back and forth
Across the whole earth
To show Yourself strong
On behalf of those
Whose hearts are in harmony with Yours.
As You search back and forth
At six o'clock each morning, dear God,
I know You see me
As I reluctantly crawl
From under the soft blankets
And stumble in the dark
Toward my living room trysting place.
It isn't easy to cater
To the clanging alarm
Especially on cold winter mornings
When my will is so weak
And the bed feels so warm.
But after an hour of meditation and prayer
You miraculously renew me
And my spirit is wonderfully restored.
Thank You for showing Yourself strong
On my behalf, dear Lord
As I sit in my brown chair
Reading Your Word and
Hearing Your voice
At six o'clock in the morning.

For the eyes of the Lord range throughout the earth to strengthen
those whose hearts are fully committed to him.   2 Chronicles 16:9, NIV

December 20

Christmas Gratitude

Lord
As I stand at the kitchen sink
Mixing batter for Christmas
    cookies
The scent of spicy pine
Permeates our house.
Already everyone is rushing in our
    town!
I remember that it started years
    ago
When the startled shepherds
Came with haste
To find the newborn Baby.

Dear God
As I bake enormous batches of
    cookies
This beautiful Christmas season
I pray for sufficient strength
To go with haste

To the frightened and lonely
To the worn and weary
To those without courage and
    hope.
Lord, may each batch of cookies
Be mixed with love—
Not just mine, but Yours!

Right now, dear God
With flour smudging my face
And dough clinging to my fingers
I praise You with all my heart
For loving us enough
To give the very best—
The gift of Your only begotten
    Son.

They ran to the village and found Mary and Joseph. And there was
the baby, lying in the manger. Then the shepherds told everyone what
had happened and what the angel had said to them about this child.

Luke 2:16-17, NLT

December 21

The Wonder of It All!

It happened at a popular department store several years ago. The store was charged with excitement. Parents and children rushed madly, pushing into elevators and slow-moving escalators. At noon Santa was coming to the store in a helicopter!

The huge clock on the main floor moved slowly. Eleven-thirty . . . eleven-forty-five . . . then five minutes to twelve. Milling crowds pushed through the doors to get to the parking lot. Hundreds of excited eyes looked skyward. Santa was on time! The joy was almost too great to bear.

Suddenly above the excitement the high-pitched voice of one little boy was heard: "Mommy, Mommy, look! Santa is waving, and he's waving to *me!*" For one little boy, Santa's wave was personal.

That's the wonder of it all! Not because we have a Santa-God, but because we have a personal God who literally stepped from eternity to take on humanity. Over against the world's darkness there is Jesus Christ, the Son of God! In every village, every city, and every faraway country, the cry of triumph can be "He came for *me!* He died for *me!* He rose for *me!*"

That's the glory of Christmas!

God so loved the world that he gave his only Son, so that everyone who believes in him will not perish but have eternal life.

John 3:16, NLT

Memories

Dear God
How I thank You
For thousands of beautiful memories
That have become a growing history
Of Your supreme goodness in my life.
Thank You for many memories
Flaming memories, trailing memories.
Thank You for throbbing memories
Quiet, gentle memories
Pink-tinted memories
That live on and on
To gladden somber days.
Thank You for memories that have rooted me
Stabilized me, sensitized me
And toughened the inner fiber of my being.
In Your honor, dear God
I erect my *Monument of Memories.*
For Your glory . . . You who are
My "living bright Reality."

I remember the days of long ago; I meditate on all your works and
consider what your hands have done. I spread out my hands to you; my
soul thirsts for you like a parched land.   Psalm 143:5-6, NIV

December 23

Explanation

Just this week

I read a newspaper account

Of a thirteen-year-old boy

Who saved his brother's life

By driving him to a hospital

In his father's car.

Never having driven before

His explanation was simple:

"I just did what I saw my father do."

O dear God

Please empower me to bring life

To a sick, wounded world

With the simple explanation:

"I do what my Father does."

The world must learn that I love the Father and that I do exactly
what my Father has commanded me.   John 14:31, NIV

December 24

The Gift

Lord

The shopping is finished

The gifts, beautifully wrapped

Are placed with gentleness

Under our smiling tree.

We chose carefully, Lord

Just the right gifts

For those who are so dear to us.

Today I am suddenly aware

That long years ago

In the fullness of time

You sent the Gift of Your Son

Because we are so dear to You!

O God, thank You!

But when the right time came, God sent his Son, born of a woman,
subject to the law. God sent him to buy freedom for us who were
slaves to the law, so that he could adopt us as his very own children.

Galatians 4:4-5, NLT

December 25

It's Christmas

It's Christmas!

Sing!
Rejoice!
Celebrate!

Let God create in you
Colorful explosions
Of joy and excitement.
Smile away fears, push away tears.
Out with pretense, in with praise.

It's Christmas!

Open your heart to light
To trust, to love, to hope.
Awaken slumbering memories
Stir up stupendous dreams
Anticipate surprises
Open your arms wide.

It's Christmas!

Time for candles and cards
For carols and cookies
For brightly lit trees

With the fragrance of pine.
Time to hug and hold
To think and thank
Time to greet the world
With the Good News.

It's Christmas!

Thank God for life
Thank Him for the manger
For the splintered cross
For the empty tomb.
Thank Him for His only Son
The Savior of the world.

Shout!
Laugh!
Share!
Care!

And say to God
On Christmas morning:
"I entrust myself anew
To You."

The Word became flesh and made his dwelling among us. We have seen his glory, the glory of the one and only Son, who came from the Father, full of grace and truth.

John 1:14, NIV

December 26

The Song I Sing

O dear God
Make me a woman of concern
And deep, deep compassion.
There is so much loneliness
So much despair and neglect
So much pain and disappointment
In the world today.
I see it all around me, Lord.
In my block, my church
In the homes of families and friends.
Make me achingly aware.
Let me care, let me share.
Lord, may I be at least one chord
Of beautiful music
In the heart of a mother
Or a father or a precious child
Where the longing for harmony
Lies so deeply hidden.
Above all, my Lord
Channel through me
Your matchless love
For You are the Song I joyfully sing.

For God, who said, "Let there be light in the darkness," has made us understand that this light is the brightness of the glory of God that is seen in the face of Jesus Christ. But this precious treasure—this light and power that now shine within us—is held in perishable containers, that is, in our weak bodies. So everyone can see that our glorious power is from God and is not our own.   2 Corinthians 4:6-7, NLT

December 27

The Promise (2 Samuel 22:29, TLB)

And the Lord will lighten my darkness . . .

O Lord, how I needed to read this promise
In Your Word this very day.
You will lighten my darkness.
You will *personally* do it.
I cannot, nor can my family.
My friends cannot
Nor can the one dearest to me.
You alone can lighten my darkness.
Though it is pitch black
Though clouds pile heavy and high
Though thunder roars
Though I see only confusion
You will lighten my darkness.
My hope is in You.
I look for You. I wait for You.
Nothing will prevent it.
You will lighten my darkness.

For you are the fountain of life, the light by which we see.

Psalm 36:9, NLT

December 28

SUNDAY
Lord, today I wish I were a cheerleader running and waving colorful pom-poms in tribute to your majesty. All of nature exalts you—from the newest blade of grass to the tallest mountain peak. And I? I lift my heart in praise for the wonder of it all.

MONDAY
Today, Lord, I asked how I could know if my surrender was complete. You said so quickly, "How is it *now,* this moment? Settle it each moment, and you won't need to ask."

TUESDAY
This afternoon at the sunny beach I sent a thousand thoughts tumbling into the crashing breakers. I heard you say, "My boundless love surrounds you. . . ."

WEDNESDAY
When I was washing windows today I was thinking how variable my life is . . . high moments and low moments. Deep joy, and then when I least expect it, a crushing blow. It happens often in my life. God, do you want to explain it or must I just keep on—you know—TRUSTING?

THURSDAY
God, you know more about my needs than I do. You know my hopes, my longings, my dreams. Even when you seem to be silent, surely it must mean that you are always in pursuit of solutions not yet apparent.

Give thanks to the Lord and proclaim his greatness. Let the whole world know what he has done. Sing to him; yes, sing his praises. Tell everyone about his miracles.

Psalm 105:1-2, NLT

December 29

I Promise You

My Father

How You will send Your help

I don't know.

But as certain as You are Love

Your help will come!

As surely as You keep Your word

You will supply my need.

I don't know what to do

But my eyes are on You.

You have said

"I promise you."

As we know Jesus better, his divine power gives us everything we need for living a godly life. He has called us to receive his own glory and goodness! And by that same mighty power, he has given us all of his rich and wonderful promises.   2 Peter 1:3-4, NLT

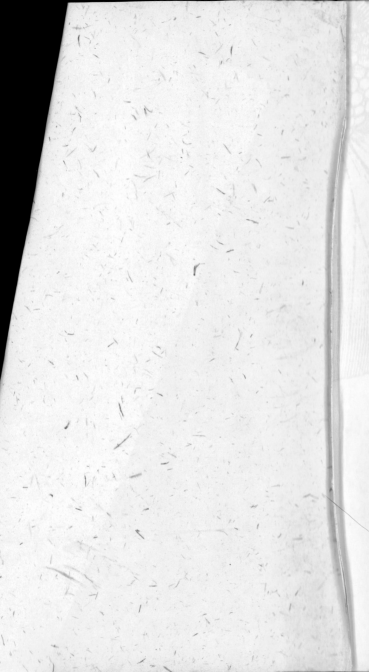

Listen Trustingly

Lord, I'm listening.

Why don't I hear You?

Fretful child

You listen

Strenuously

Anxiously

Laboriously.

Rest in Me

And listen

Trustingly.

I am talking

All the time.

But the Counselor, the Holy Spirit, whom the Father will send in my name, will teach you all things and will remind you of everything I have said to you. Peace I leave with you; my peace I give you. I do not give to you as the world gives. Do not let your hearts be troubled and do not be afraid.   John 14:26-27, NIV

December 31

Day of Rejoicing

Lord, all day long

We've been laughing and singing.

We've been shouting and praising.

After weeks and months

Of waiting and pleading

You have wonderfully answered our prayers.

Our hearts are filled with unspeakable joy.

You promised that those

Who sow in tears

Shall reap in joy.

It is happening, dear Lord

To us . . . to *us!*

Those who sow in tears will reap with songs of joy. He who goes out weeping, carrying seed to sow, will return with songs of joy, carrying sheaves with him.　　　　　Psalm 126:5-6, NIV

December 31

Day of Rejoicing

Lord, all day long

We've been laughing and singing.

We've been shouting and praising.

After weeks and months

Of waiting and pleading

You have wonderfully answered our prayers.

Our hearts are filled with unspeakable joy.

You promised that those

Who sow in tears

Shall reap in joy.

It is happening, dear Lord

To us . . . to *us!*

Those who sow in tears will reap with songs of joy. He who goes out weeping, carrying seed to sow, will return with songs of joy, carrying sheaves with him.

Psalm 126:5-6, NIV

December 30

Listen Trustingly

Lord, I'm listening.

Why don't I hear You?

Fretful child

You listen

Strenuously

Anxiously

Laboriously.

Rest in Me

And listen

Trustingly.

I am talking

All the time.

But the Counselor, the Holy Spirit, whom the Father will send in my name, will teach you all things and will remind you of everything I have said to you. Peace I leave with you; my peace I give you. I do not give to you as the world gives. Do not let your hearts be troubled and do not be afraid.

John 14:26-27, NIV